THE JEWISH RELIGION ETHICALLY PRESENTED

HENRY PEREIRA MENDES

CONTENTS

Preface   I

PART I

THE JEWISH RELIGION.
1. Religion and the Bible   7

THE SHEMA'.
2. First Section: Love   13
3. Our Confession Of Faith   14
4. The Kingdom Of God   16
5. Duty To Our God; Or God's Love For Us And Our Love For Him   18
6. Duty To Ourselves, Love To God, Religion In Our Hearts   20
7. Love For God In Speech   22
8. Love For God In Action And Thought   25
9. Love For God In Home, Social And Public Life   27
10. Justice   29
11. Holiness   31

HOLY DAYS AND FESTIVALS
12. The Sabbath.   37
13. New Year (Rosh Hashana)   41
14. The Day Of Atonement (Kippur)   43
15. The Three Festivals   46
16. The Second Festival   49
17. Succoth, or the Festival of Tabernacles   52

THE MINOR FESTIVALS.
18. Hanukah.   57
19. Purim   59
20. The Minor Fasts   61

THE TEN COMMANDMENTS.

21. The First Commandment.	65
22. The Second Commandment	69
23. The Third Commandment	71
24. The Fourth Commandment	73
25. The Fifth Commandment	75
26. The Sixth Commandment	77
27. The Seventh Commandment	79
28. The Eighth Commandment	81
29. The Ninth Commandment	84
30. The Tenth Commandment	87

PART II

THE CREED.

31. The Meaning of the Creeds	95
32. The First Creed.	96
33. The Second Creed.	99
34. The Third Creed.	102
35. The Fourth Creed.	104
36. The Fifth Creed.	107
37. The Sixth Creed.	112
38. The Seventh Creed.	115
39. The Eighth Creed.	118
40. The Ninth Creed.	120
41. The Tenth Creed.	121
42. The Eleventh Creed.	123
43. The Twelfth Creed.	127
44. The Thirteenth Creed.	133

LAWS.

45. Laws Of Conduct, Or Moral Laws And Ethical Teachings	141
46. Ceremonial Law (continued)	152
47. NAMING OF GIRLS.	154

HOME PRAYERS AND CONDUCT REMINDERS.

48. THE READING OF HOME PRAYERS. THE SHEMA', (KERIATH SHEMA',).	159
49. GRACE BEFORE AND AFTER MEALS.	161
50. THE LIGHTING OF THE SABBATH LAMP BY THE MOTHER. (Hadlakath Ha-ner).	163

51. THE SANCTIFICATION OF THE SABBATH BY THE FATHER (Kiddush).	164
52. THE "DIVISION" (Havdalah), OR CONSECRATION OF THE SENSES FOR THE COMING WEEK'S WORK.	165
53. Conduct—Reminders. The Fringe. (Tsitsith)	166
54. THE PHYLACTERIES (Tephillin).	167
55. THE DOOR-POST INSCRIPTION (Mezuzah).	169
56. Bar-Mitzvah And The Passage From Childhood To Youth—Confirmation	170
57. THE RELIGIOUS EDUCATION OF BOYS AND GIRLS.	172
58. CONSECRATION OF THE HOME (Chinuch-Habayith).	175
59. Kaddish Or Memorial Prayer	176
60. HAGOMEL OR BLESSING FOR RECOVERY FROM SICKNESS OR FOR ESCAPE FROM ANY GREAT DANGER.	177
61. PRIVATE PRAYER IN SYNAGOGUE OR TEMPLE.	178
62. The Dietary Laws	179
63. The Attitude Of Judaism To Christianity	182

APPENDICES

Appendix I.	193
Appendix II.	195
Appendix III.	197
Appendix IV.	199
Appendix V.	201

PREFACE

To the General Reader.

The object of this book is character-building.

Nothing can build character more nobly than the Jewish religion.

But its ethical aspect must be presented and studied if this, its real purpose, is to be successfully effected.

I have in this little work merely attempted to indicate how every enactment and every ceremony of our beloved religion is designed to develop our better or spiritual nature, or as I have already expressed it, to build character.

To Parents.

Home example is the most potent. The reverential (I emphasize *reverential*) discharge of sacred duties, such as home prayers, and religious ceremonies, combined with interest in the children's religious education, will go far to build up sterling manhood and womanhood.

The mother who understands her holy privilege will herself hear her children recite their little prayers, and by judicious praise or rebuke, mould their characters at the most impressionable moments.

And the father can best discharge his most sacred responsibilities of fatherhood by personally conducting home devotions at appropriate seasons.

To Rabbis or Ministers.

I have presented Judaism from the ethical standpoint. I am confident that all Jewish ministers will welcome any presentation whose object is character building on the lines of Reverence, Faith, Love, Justice and Holiness, with our Bible for foundation.

Where I have drawn upon rabbinical or other ancient sources and ancient prayers, will be recognized. But I have chiefly drawn naturally and purposely, upon the Bible. For that is our Book of Books, and the very reason for my copious quotations therefrom is my earnest desire to make the People of the Book better acquainted with the Book of the People.

To Teachers.

An asterisk (*) divides each chapter. Up to the asterisk is for young children. From the asterisk to the end of the chapter is for older boys and girls.

The paragraphs in each chapter are numbered. The teacher therefore can exercise his discretion in selecting lessons according to the capacity of the class.

The Bible quotations are numbered to correspond with the paragraphs, which they illustrate, and to which they refer.

These quotations should be read frequently in class *and some should be memorized each week.*

The main object of the quotations is to saturate the children with Bible verses in Bible language.

Chapter XLIV. is entirely Bible Quotations. The teacher will select some from time to time for study, for class-discussion or for class-talks.

Recitations of quotations at every session of the class should be encouraged. A class quotation, like a class motto, may be selected for each year.

That is to say, the words of the Bible should be woven into the very warp and woof of life. They should be creators of conduct. They should be *builders of character*.

That is what our religion is meant to be.

PART I

THE JEWISH RELIGION.

1

RELIGION AND THE BIBLE

1. Religion means our duty to God, our duty to our fellow-beings and our duty to ourselves.

2. God is the Great and Good Being, who made the heavens and all the worlds that are in them, the earth and all that is in it. He loves us and desires us all to be perfect, that is, to act righteously.

3. We can be truly righteous only by doing what God wishes us to do.

4. We learn about religion, or what God wishes us to do, chiefly in a book called the Bible.

5. The Bible contains laws of conduct which God has lovingly given to us to guide us in all our duties, so that our lives may be happy and our conduct righteous.

6. The Bible also contains our history for fifteen hundred years, and God's messages to all mankind.

*[1]7. The Bible is divided into:

The Torah (the Law), or five books of Moses, sometimes called the Pentateuch.
Nevi-im (the Prophets).
Ketuvim (Holy Writings).

8. The five books of Moses are Genesis, Exodus, Leviticus, Numbers and Deuteronomy.

9. Genesis means creation. This book contains the story of the creation of the world, also early events in human history, and the history of our patriarchs or first teachers of our religion, Abraham, Isaac and Jacob.

10. Exodus means departure. It contains the story of the departure from

Egypt, also the revelation of the ten commandments, and describes the erection of the Tabernacle where people might seek the Lord in communion. (For Communion, what it means, see *chapter xxxvi. 8, Part II*).

11. Leviticus contains laws concerning the Levites, or priestly tribe; food-laws and health-laws for all, with Holydays and Festivals, land-laws, etc.

12. Numbers contains the census or numbering of the people, and the story of the Hebrews' forty years sojourn in the wilderness before they entered Palestine, the Holy Land.

13. Deuteronomy means Repetition. It contains the last addresses of Moses to the people, in which he repeated the chief laws and reminded them of certain events in their history. This book also contains the witness-song of Moses and his blessing upon Israel.

14. In the Nevi-im, or Prophets, are ten books, six older and four later. The older books are Joshua, Judges, 1st and 2nd Samuel, 1st and 2nd Kings. The later books are Isaiah, Jeremiah, Ezekiel and the books of the minor prophets, so called because their books are smaller. Being so small, they are all reckoned together as one book. Their names are Hosea, Joel, Amos, Obadiah, Jonah, Micah, Nahum, Habakuk, Zephaniah, Haggai, Zachariah and Malachi.

15. In the Ketuvim, or Holy Writings, are nine books, as follows: Psalms, Proverbs, Job, the Five Rolls (Ruth, Song of Solomon, Ecclesiastes, Lamentations of Jeremiah, Esther), Daniel, Ezra, Nehemiah, 1st and 2nd Books of Chronicles.

～

BIBLE QUOTATIONS.[2]
Our Duty to God

1. And now, O Israel, what doth the Lord thy lord require of thee but to revere the Lord thy God, to walk In all His ways and to love and to serve the Lord thy God with all thy heart and with all thy soul.—Deut. x, 12.

And thou shalt love the Lord thy God with all thy heart, and with all thy soul and with all thy might.—Deut. vi, 5.

Fear (revere) God and keep His commandments, for this is the whole duty of man.—Eccles. xii, 13.

Our Duty to Our Fellow-Beings

Be a blessing.—Gen. xii, 2.

Thou shalt love thy neighbor as thyself.—Leviticus xix, 18.

One statute, one law, one judgment, shall be for you and for the stranger that sojourneth with you.—Numbers xv, 15, 16.

Ye shall love the stranger.—Deut. x, 19.

Our Duty to Ourselves.

Be perfect with the Lord thy God.—Deut. xviii, 13.

Sanctify yourselves and be holy.—Levit. xi, 44.

Be ye holy for Me, for I, the Lord, am holy, and I have separated you from the peoples to be for Me (to stand for He).—Levit. xx, 26.

Ye shall not mar yourselves, * * * thou shalt not eat any vile food.—Deut. xiv, 1-3.

2. Thou art the only Lord. Thou didst make the heaven the heaven of heavens and all their host, the earth and all that is thereon, the waters and all that is therein. Thou dost give life to them all, and the hosts of heaven worship Thee.—Nehem. ix, 6.

For the Lord thy God loveth thee.—Deut. xxiii, 6.

Walk before Me and be perfect.—Gen. xvii, 1.

3. And it shall be our righteousness, when we are careful to perform all this commandment before the Lord our God, as He hath commanded us.—Deut. vi, 25.

4. These are the statutes and the judgments and the laws which the Lord gave.—Levit. xxvi, 46.

I speak by the prophets.—Hosea xi, 11.

5. Observe most carefully the commands of the Lord your God, and His testimonies and His statutes which He hath commanded thee. And thou shalt do what is right and good in the eyes of the Lord in order that thou mayst be happy.—Deut. vi, 17, 18.

To make known Thy ways on earth, Thy salvation among the nations.—Psalm lxvii, 2.

---

1. For explanation of the asterisk (*) see Preface
2. The Bible quotations are numbered to correspond with the paragraphs in the preceding chapter. They should be read after the paragraph to which they thus refer and which they illustrate.

THE SHEMA'.

2

FIRST SECTION: LOVE

(This chapter is for older children.)

1. The Shema', so called from the first word of the Hebrew text, is recited by us on rising and on retiring every day, because it declares our confession of Faith and our religious duty.

2. The declaration or confession of our faith is that THE LORD IS OUR GOD and that HE IS THE ONE AND ONLY GOD.

3. Our chief religious duty is to love Him with a whole-hearted, whole-souled and mighty love.

4. This love is to inspire our hearts (verse 4); we are to teach it to our children most impressively (v. 5); it must influence our speech at all times (v. 5); it must guide the acts of our hands (v. 6); it must direct our very thoughts (v. 6); it must pervade our home life (v. 7), and it must rule our social, business or public life (v. 7).

5. If we love God with such a perfect love, we will never do anything to displease Him, we will try always to please Him, and we will thus obey Him willingly, joyously and enthusiastically.

[For Bible quotations, see Appendix.]

3

OUR CONFESSION OF FAITH

First verse of the Shema':
**Hear, O Israel, the Lord is our God,
the Lord is one.**

1. The Lord alone is our God.
2. There is no God besides Him.
3. To Him alone may we pray.
4. He alone can save us, protect us, help us and bless us.
5. We prove that the Lord is our God by obeying Him and honoring Him always.
6. It is no use saying that the Lord is our God unless we always do what He wishes us, and unless we always try to please Him.
*7. Since He is the only God, we are responsible to Him alone.
8. If we sin, He alone can forgive us.
9. To pray to any other Being, or to ask pardon from any other Being, is to insult His honor and to profane His Holy Name.
10. The knowledge that we are directly responsible to Him alone should lead us to realize that although He is our Judge, He is also our loving and merciful Father in Heaven.

BIBLE QUOTATIONS.

1. Know therefore this day and reflect in thy heart, that the Lord He is God in heaven above and on the earth beneath; there is none else.—Deut. iv, 40.
2. I am the Lord, and there is none else, there is no God besides Me.—Isa. xlv, 5.

3. Look unto Me, and be ye saved, all the ends of the earth, for I am God and there is none else.—Isa. xlv, 22.

4. I, even I, am the Lord, and besides Me there is no Savior.—Isa. xliii, 11.

Ye that revere the Lord, trust in the Lord; He is their help and shield.—Psalm cxv, 11.

God, even our own God, will bless us.—Psalm lxvii, 7.

7. Against Thee, Thee only, have I sinned.—Psalm li, 4.

8. Forgiveness is with Thee.—Psalm cxxx, 4.

9. I am the Lord: that is My name; and My glory I will not give to another.—Isa. xlii, 8.

10. But now, O Lord, Thou art our Father. . . . Be not wroth very sore, O Lord, neither remember iniquity forever.—Isa. xliv. 8, 9.

4

THE KINGDOM OF GOD

Second verse of the Shema':
**Blessed be the name of the Glory of
His Kingdom for ever and ever.**

1. God is our King. The Hebrew word for king means one who guides or leads.
2. God is our king who guides or leads us.
3. His kingdom will be established on earth when all mankind will follow His guidance. All will then be happy, for men will then act righteously.
4. The glory of any king is the happiness of his subjects. So the glory of God, who is the supreme King of Kings, is the happiness of His creatures. God desires that we, His creatures, should be happy, because He loves us. But human happiness cannot exist without righteousness.
5. We help to establish God's kingdom on earth and to spread its glory, when we try to promote each other's happiness, and when we promote righteousness in every way possible.
*6. "*The name* of the glory of His kingdom" means the nature, the existence, the establishment of the glory of His kingdom.
7. Therefore, when we pray "Blessed be the name of the glory of His kingdom" we mean "Blessed be the establishment of the glory of God's kingdom on earth."
8. The establishment of God's kingdom means the time when men will not try to injure each other. Righteousness will rule human life. There will be no violence, no cruelty. Even nations, instead of fighting, will go before judges to have their disputes decided. All men, all nations, will obey the laws of the Lord, our God, and will be guided by Him, the King of the Universe.

9. The establishment of God's kingdom on earth is what we mean by the Messianic Era, or Era of Peace and Righteousness. See *Chapter xlii (Part II)*.

[NOTE.—*This verse is not in Deuteronomy. It is what our ancestors used to say when they heard God's sacred Name solemnly pronounced in the Temple on certain special occasions.*]

BIBLE QUOTATIONS.

1. The Lord is King; let the earth rejoice.—Psalm xcvii, 1.
God is King of all the earth.—Psalm xlvii, 6.
The kingdom is the Lord's, and He is Ruler over all nations.—Psalm xxii, 28.
Thine is the kingdom, O Lord.—1 Chron. xxix, 11.
They shall speak of the glory of Thy Kingdom, and talk of Thy power.—Psalm cxlv, 11.
He guided thee in the wilderness.—Deut. viii, 15.
2. He is our Guide even unto death.—Psalm xlviii, 14.
3. And the Lord shall be King over all the earth.—Zech. xiv, 9.
Unto Me every knee shall bend.—Isa. xlv, 23.
All nations which Thou hast made shall come and worship before Thee, O Lord, and shall honor Thy Name.—Psalm lxxxv, 9.
4. Who is this King of glory? The Lord of Hosts, He is the King of glory.—Psalm xxiv, 10.
Glory shall dwell in our land. . . . Yea, the Lord will give happiness.—Psalm lxxxv, 9-11.
The whole earth shall be filled with His glory.—Psalm lxxiii, 19.
5. Make your ways and your doings good.—Jerem. xviii, 11.
Do good.—Psalm xxxiv, 14.
Seek peace and pursue it.—Psalm xxxiv, 14.
Seek good and not evil, that ye may live.—Amos v, 14.
Hate evil, love what is the good and establish justice.—Amos v, 15.
Show loving kindness and compassion every one to his brother.—Zech. vii, 9.
Oppress not the widow, nor the fatherless, nor the stranger, nor the poor, and let none of you imagine evil in his heart against his brother.—Zech. vii, 10.
Speak ye every man the truth to his neighbor.—Zech. viii, 16.
6. All flesh shall bless *the name* of His holiness for ever and ever.—Psalm xlv, 21.
8. Glory shall dwell in our land. Mercy and Truth shall meet, Righteousness and Peace shall embrace. Truth shall spring forth from earth and charity shall look down from Heaven. Yea, the Lord will give happiness.—Psalm lxxxv, 9-11.

5

DUTY TO OUR GOD; OR GOD'S LOVE FOR US AND OUR LOVE FOR HIM

Third verse of the Shema':
**And thou shalt love the Lord thy God,
with all thy heart, and with all thy soul,
and with all thy might.**

1. God loves us. Therefore we must love Him.
2. His love provides everything for our happiness. He made the beautiful earth in which we live. He gives us parents and friends to love and take care of us, food for our nourishment and work for us to do.
3. Because He loves us with such great love, we must love Him in return "with all our heart, with all our soul and with all our might," and we must teach others to love Him.
4. To love God "with all our heart" means to love Him so dearly that we are happy only when we feel that we possess His love. And when, if we do wrong, we are unhappy until we ask His pardon and thus obtain His love again.
5. We are happy when we do what is right, and unhappy if we do what is wrong. This feeling tells us whether we possess His love or not.
6. We must therefore always try to please Him, in order to deserve His love, and never to displease Him, lest we lose it.
7. To love God "with all our soul" means to love Him so sincerely that we will willingly die sooner than do what He forbids us.
8. To love Him "with all our might" means that we must use all our powers to serve Him and do His will.
*9. "His will be done" is a pious prayer. When we do His will and not ours, then we prove that we love Him with all our heart.

10. We love God with all our heart when we give Him a whole-hearted and not a half-hearted love.

11. For a half-hearted love will mean a half-hearted obedience.

12. Those who give up their lives for the sake of religion, or in order to perform God's will, are called Martyrs.

13. If so many of our ancestors gave up their lives for the sake of religion, ought not we to be willing to give up convenience or earthly gain for God's sake?

14. Love is proved by sacrifice. That is, we prove our love for anyone by the sacrifices we are willing to make for him or her.

15. The strength of our love for God is proved by the greatness of the sacrifices we are willing to make for Him.

BIBLE QUOTATIONS.
GOD'S LOVE FOR US.

1. The Lord thy God loveth thee.—Deut. xxiii, 5.
He loveth the stranger.—Deut. x, 18.
Yea, He loveth the peoples.—Deut. xxxiii, 3.
With everlasting love, I love thee.—Jerem. xxxi, 3.

OUR LOVE FOR GOD.

2. And thou shalt love the Lord thy God with all thy heart and with all thy soul and with all thy might.—Deut. vi, 5.

I love the Lord.—Psalm cxvi, 1.

And now, Israel, what doth the Lord thy God require of thee but to revere the Lord thy God, to walk in all His ways, and to love Him, and to serve the Lord thy God with all thy heart and with all thy soul, to keep the commandments of the Lord and His statutes which I command thee this day for thy good?—Deut. x, 12-13.

3. What can I render unto the Lord for all His benefits toward me?—Psalm cxvi, 12.

9. Do thou unto us whatsoever seemeth good unto Thee.—Judges x, 15.

Let the Lord do to me as seemeth good unto Him.—II. Sam. xv, 26.

11. To love the Lord your God with all your heart and with all your soul.—Deut. xi, 13.

14. Now, therefore, I pray thee, let thy servant abide instead of the lad a bondman to my lord, and let the lad go up with his brethren.—Genesis xliv, 33.

O my son, Absalom, my son, my son, Absalom! Would to God I had died for thee, Absalom, my son, my son!—II. Sam. xviii, 33.

6

DUTY TO OURSELVES, LOVE TO GOD, RELIGION IN OUR HEARTS

Fourth verse of the Shema':
And these words which I command thee this day, shall be upon thy heart.

1. The words which are to be upon our hearts are the words: "Thou shalt love the Lord thy God with all thy heart, and with all thy soul, and with all thy might."
2. It means that a real love for God must rule our hearts.
3. Merely saying that we love Him is not enough.
4. Our conduct, what we do, and what we say, and what we think, must prove it.
5. If we really love God with all our heart, with all our soul, and with all our might, we will then do all that our religion commands us. For we will then never do anything to displease Him. We will surely do everything to please Him.
*6. Real love for God can only exist in a pure heart. For an impure heart will have in it love for self or love for gain. Love for God will then be lessened or altogether destroyed.
7. Wrong thoughts make an impure heart.
8. Even if we cannot help wrong thoughts coming to us, we can, and must, prevent them remaining in our hearts.
9. We must not allow ourselves to indulge in wicked thoughts.
10. For wicked thoughts drive love for God out of our hearts.

BIBLE QUOTATIONS.

2. The Lord looketh on the heart.—I. Sam. xvi, 7.

3. My heart, my whole being, crieth out for the living God.—Psalm lxxxiv, 2.

4. The Lord your God proveth you, to know whether ye love the Lord your God with all your heart and with all your soul.—Deut. xiii, 3.

Make me to go in the path of Thy commandments; for, therein do I delight.—Psalm cxix, 35.

May the words of my mouth and the meditation of my heart be acceptable in Thy sight.—Psalm xix, 14.

5. I will delight myself in Thy commandments, which I have loved.—Psalm cxix, 47.

6. Create in me a clean heart, O God, and renew a right spirit within me.—Psalm li, 10.

8. (The Lord hateth) the heart that thinketh wicked thoughts.—Prov. vi, 18.

9. The thought of folly is sin.—Prov. xxiv, 9.

7

LOVE FOR GOD IN SPEECH

Fifth verse of the Shema':
**And thou shalt teach them
diligently unto thy children;
And thou shalt speak of them
when thou sittest in thy house
and when thou walkest by the way,
and when thou liest down**

1. God commands parents to teach their children to love Him with all their heart, with all their soul and with all their might.

2. Therefore we must honor our parents and love them because they teach us what is necessary for our right conduct.

3. We must speak of our love for God and prove that it is real and influences our conduct at all times.

4. Our love for God should make us have love in our homes.

5. Our love for God should influence our conduct out of our homes.

6. Our love for God should, when we retire, make us grateful for all His love and protection during the day that has passed. It is also wise to examine our conduct of the day, before closing our eyes, feeling that God is judging our self-examination.

7. Our love for God should, when we rise up, make us trust in Him for His help and blessing during the day which is beginning. Nor should we forget to be grateful for His loving care of our dear ones and of ourselves during the night.

*8. The duty of parents to give their children a religious education is frequently repeated in the Bible. Because, without religious education, our characters cannot be fully developed. We will become selfish, worldly and unsympathetic.

9. A religious education trains us to do our duty to God, to man and to ourselves.

10. Our duty to God is to know Him, to reverence Him, to love Him and to serve Him.

11. Our duty to man is to love our neighbor as ourselves and never to do to him what we would not like him to do to us.

12. Our duty to ourselves is to get the best education possible in religion and in all subjects, to take care of our health and never to lose the respect of our neighbors or our own self-respect.

13. We know God by studying what the Bible and Nature around us tell us about Him, and by our own experiences of His justice and goodness.

14. We reverence Him when we think how great He is and how little we are, how good and forbearing He is and how unworthy of His love we often are.

15. We love Him when our conduct proves our desire to please Him, through the sacrifices we make for Him.

16. We serve Him when we perform the duties He gives us.

17. Our knowledge, reverence, love and service of God are often expressed by prayer.

18. Prayer can be praise, thanksgiving or supplication.

19. Praise of God means declaring His greatness or majesty.

20. Thanksgiving to God means acknowledgment of His goodness.

21. Supplication to God means asking His help or pardon.

BIBLE QUOTATIONS.

2. Honor thy father and thy mother.—Ex. xx, 12.

7. To declare Thy loving kindness in the morning and Thy faithfulness in the night.—Psalm xcii. 2.

10. Let him that glorieth glory in this, that he understandeth and knoweth Me, that I am the Lord who exerciseth loving kindness, judgment and righteousness on earth; for in these things I delight, saith the Lord.—Jerem. x, 24.

And now, Israel, what doth the Lord require of thee, but to revere the Lord thy God, to walk in all His ways, and to love Him, and to serve the Lord thy God with all thy heart and with all thy soul; to keep the commandments of the Lord, and His statutes, which I command thee this day for thy happiness?—Deut. x, 12-13.

11. Thou shalt love thy neighbor as thyself.—Lev. xix, 18.

12. Take heed to thyself and keep thy soul diligently.—Deut. iv, 9.

13. Lift up your eyes on high, and behold who hath created these things, that bringeth out their host by number: He calleth them all by names, by the greatness of His might and that He is strong in power; not one faileth.—Isa. xl, 26.

14. I am unworthy of the least of all the kindnesses and the truth which Thou hast done for Thy servant.—Gen. xxxii, 10.

19. O Lord, how manifold are Thy works! In wisdom hast Thou made them all; the Earth is full of Thy possessions.—Psalm civ, 24.

20. O give thanks unto the Lord, for He is good, for His loving kindness endureth for ever.—Psalm cxxxvi, 1.

21. Hear my prayer, O God.—Psalm liv, 2.

8

LOVE FOR GOD IN ACTION AND THOUGHT

Sixth verse of the Shema':
**And thou shalt bind them
for a sign upon thy hand and
they shall be as frontlets between thine eyes.**

1. We are to bind the words "And thou shalt love the Lord thy God with all thy heart, and with all thy soul and with all thy might" upon our hands and between our eyes.
2. This means that love for God must influence what we do with our hands and what we think with our brains.
3. Frontlets, in ancient times, were ornaments worn upon the forehead.
4. This and the last verse together teach us that our love for God must make us speak, do, and think what is right.
*5. Wearing the Shema', etc., as a frontlet thus becomes a reminder of Right Conduct through love of God.
6. This verse is the origin of the use of the Tephillin or phylacteries.
7. The Tephillin contain four sections of the Law, which set forth all that is dear and holy in the Jewish Religion. See *chapter xlvii, No. 9 (Part II.)*
8. They are worn, therefore, because of what they teach and because of their influence when rightly understood, upon conduct, just as the High Priest wore on his forehead the inscription "Holy to the Lord," to teach holiness as the ideal of human conduct.
9. Hence the ancient meditation, recited when about to wear Tephillin, "Through the influence of this command, the Tephillin, may we be blessed with sacred impulses and hallowing thoughts, with no thought of sin or iniq-

uity. May evil imagination have no power to allure us and lead us astray, but may we be led to worship the Lord as it is in our hearts to do."

BIBLE QUOTATIONS.

2. God cometh to prove you, and in order that His fear may be before your eyes, that ye sin not.—Exod. xx, 20.

4. For thou shalt hearken unto the voice of the Lord thy God, to keep all His commandments which I command thee this day, to do that which is right in the eyes of the Lord.—Deut. xiii, 18.

Keep thy tongue from evil and thy lips from speaking guile.—Psalm xxxiv, 13.

I will meditate upon Thy precepts, and I will discern Thy ways.—Psalm cxix, 15.

May my heart be perfect in Thy statutes, so that I be not shamed.—Psalm cxix, 80.

Lead me O Lord, in Thy righteousness.—Psalm v, 8.

Cause me to know the way wherein I should walk.—Psalm cxliii, 8.

9

LOVE FOR GOD IN HOME, SOCIAL AND PUBLIC LIFE

Seventh verse of the Shema':
**And thou shalt write them
on the door-posts of thy house
and upon thy gates.**

1. We are to write the words "And thou shalt love the Lord thy God," etc., on the door-posts of our homes to remind us that love for God must govern our conduct to those who are therein and must direct our own private life.

2. We prove our love for God, therefore, by honoring our parents, by respecting the aged, by attention to our teachers, by kindness to brothers and sisters, by helping the poor who come to us, by consideration for our servants, in accordance with His commands, for we meet all these in our homes.

3. To write the words on our gates means that love for God must guide us in public life.

4. In ancient times many public duties were performed in the space near the gates of the city. "In the gates" means the public place.

5. The command means that in all our business as men and women, and in all our duties as citizens, we must do the right, out of love for God who so commands us.

*6. Writing these words "on the door-posts of our houses" is the origin of the custom of the Mezuzah.

7. Mezuzah is the Hebrew word for door-post. The word is used to mean the little scroll on which the first and second portions of the Shema' are written. The scroll is enclosed in a case which is fastened to the door-post.

8. Shaddai, meaning Almighty, one of the names of God, is written on the

outside, to remind us as we enter or leave the house, that God is all-mighty, and therefore we must trust in His protection.

9. Just as a flag over a house shows the loyalty of its inmates to their country, so a Mezuzah on the door-post of a house shows the loyalty of the inmates to God and to their religion.

10. The object of the Mezuzah is thus further expressed: "When we enter or leave the house, let us remember God and His love; let us be roused from the vanities of the world and realize that nought is stable save the knowledge of the Rock of the Universe. We will at once turn to that knowledge of Him and we will walk in the ways of uprightness." (Maimonides).

BIBLE QUOTATIONS.

2. Honor thy father and thy mother.—Deut. v, 16.

Thou shalt rise up before the hoary head and thou shalt honor the old.—Lev. xix, 32.

Ask thy father and he will shew thee, thine elders and they will tell thee.—Deut. xxxii, 7.

Hear me now therefore, O ye children . . . . . Lest thou sayest, How have I hated instruction, and my heart despised reproof, and have not obeyed the voice of my teachers, nor inclined mine ear to them that instructed me.—Prov. v, 7, 12, 13.

Thou shalt not hate thy brother in thy heart.—Levit. xix, 17.

Thou shalt open thine hand wide unto thy brother, to thy poor, and to thy needy in thy land.—Deut. xv, 11.

Thou shalt not oppress a hired servant that is poor and needy, whether he be of thy brethren, or of thy strangers that are in thy land within thy gates.—Deut. xxiv, 14.

5. Ye shall not steal, neither deal falsely, neither lie one to another. Thou shalt not defraud thy neighbor, neither rob him.—Lev. xix, 11-13.

Righteousness, righteousness, shalt thou pursue.—Deut. xvi, 20.

Thou shalt not raise a false report.—Exod. xxiii, 1.

Help not the wicked, to be a witness of violence.—Exod. xxiii, 1.

Follow not the multitude to do evil.—Exod. xxiii, 2.

Speak not for a contest to turn after many to wrest *right*.—Exod. xxiii, 2.

10

JUSTICE

Second Section of the Shema'.

*1. The second section of the Shema' is from Deuteronomy xi, 13-22. (See *Appendix II.*)

2. It teaches us that God rewards us if we love and serve Him with all our heart and soul, but that we must suffer if we turn away from Him.

3. We often notice that the righteous have sorrow and that the wicked are prosperous. God is the Judge and He is a righteous Judge. Therefore we may be sure that if reward for righteousness and the penalty for wrong-doing be not given by Him in this life, it will be given in the future life.

4. Hence this second section of the Shema' reminds us of Future Life.

5. We sometimes call the belief in Future Life the Doctrine of the Immortality of the Soul. *(See chapters xli-xlii.)*

BIBLE QUOTATIONS.

2. Say ye to the righteous that it shall be well with him, for they shall eat the fruit of their doings. Woe unto the wicked, it shall be ill with him, for the reward of his hands shall be given him.—Isa. iii, 10-11.

God will bring every work into judgment, whether it be good or whether it be evil.—Eccles. xii, 14.

3. Many are the afflictions of the righteous; but the Lord delivereth him out of them all.—Psalm xxxiv, 19.

Wherefore do the wicked live, become old, yea, are mighty in power?—Job xxi, 7.

Shall evil be recompensed for good?—Jerem. xviii, 20.
God is the Judge.—Psalm lxxvii, 7.

11

HOLINESS

The Third Section of the Shema'.

1. The third section of the Shema' is from Numbers xv, 37 to end. (See *Appendix III*.)
2. This section teaches us Obedience and Holiness.
3. It commands us to wear fringes in order to remind us to perform all God's commands, and to be Holy to the Lord our God.
4. It is not enough to remember God's commands. We must perform them.
5. To be holy means to lead pure lives and therefore to avoid sin.
6. Sin makes life impure or unholy.
7. The fringes are fastened to a small garment, which is worn always, or to a special garment used during prayer.
8. We wear the fringes (Tsitsith) to remind us of our duty, just as a man, wears his uniform or a woman wears her wedding-ring.
*9. To be holy *to* the Lord our God, means also to be holy *for* the Lord our God.
10. We must therefore not only be holy. We must do what is holy, and we must speak what is holy—for His sake. We must be witnesses for the Holy God.
11. Therefore "to be holy" really means the consecration of ourselves, or our lives, for God's work or purposes.
12. We consecrate ourselves in our duty to God and man when we stand for the right always.
13. The flag of our country calls upon us to make every sacrifice for its honor and integrity, and to stand for them at all times. The fringe calls upon us to make every sacrifice for its honor and integrity, and to stand for them at all

times. The fringe calls upon us to make every sacrifice for the honor and integrity of our religion, and to stand for them always.

14. We consecrate ourselves and our lives in our duty to God when we have the moral courage to perform our religious duties at all cost, and to stand for God and the Right.

15. We consecrate ourselves and our lives in our duty to our fellow beings when we have the moral courage to speak out for what is right and pure, to speak out against what is wrong and impure, and always to do the right, cost what it may, in all our dealings with mankind.

16. We consecrate ourselves and our lives in our duty to ourselves when we have the moral courage to correct our own faults, to strive after high and noble ideals, to withdraw from unworthy or wicked companionship, to persevere in the right, no matter how many times we fail in our efforts to succeed, to scorn to make a false excuse and refuse to tell a lie, to hate to say or do anything mean.

17. Sin soils the soul. We cannot consecrate ourselves to God if our souls are stained with sin, or if "we go astray."

The lessons of the Tsitsith may therefore thus be summed up:—Impure thoughts defile the heart; impure deeds defile the hands; impure words defile the lips. Any defilement is unholiness. We must be holy.

18. The ethical value of the Tsitsith is further indicated in the ancient meditation recited before using it: "Behold me enwrapping myself with the Tsitsith. O so do Thou enwrap my soul and my body in the spiritual light thereof."

19. The fringe is made in a special way to remind us of the Lord:—

20. In Hebrew all letters stand for numbers. The letters in the word for "Lord," or in the phrase "the Lord is one," thus make twenty-six or thirty-nine. A thread is therefore wound round the fringe twenty-six times by the Sephardic Jews, and thirty-nine times by the Ashkenaz Jews, to remind us of the Lord, or that He is One.

21. The Sephardic Jews are those descended from the Jews of Spain, Portugal, South-France and all other countries round the Mediterranean Sea.

22. All other Jews are called Ashkenaz Jews, and include Germans, Poles, Hungarians, Russians, Roumanians, etc.

BIBLE QUOTATIONS.

3. And it shall be unto you for a fringe, that ye may look upon it, and remember all the commandments of the Lord, and do them, and that ye seek not after your own heart and your own eyes after which ye go astray.—Numbers xvi, 39.

4. That ye may remember and do all My commandments, and be holy to your God.—Numbers xv, 40.

5. For I am the Lord your God; ye shall therefore sanctify yourselves, and ye shall be holy; for I am holy.—Levit. xii, 44.

6. Wickedness destroys the wicked.—Psalm xxxiv, 21.

9. Thou art My servant, O Israel, by whom I will be glorified.—Isa. xlix, 3.

10. Ye are My witnesses, saith the Lord, and My servants whom I have chosen.—Isa. xliii, 10.

This people have I formed for Myself; they shall show forth My praise.—Isa. xliii, 21.

11. I, the Lord, have called thee in righteousness, and will hold thine hand and will keep thee, and give thee for a covenant of the people, for a light for the Gentiles.—Isa. xlii, 6.

12. Have not I commanded thee? Be strong and of good courage; be not afraid, neither be thou dismayed; for the Lord thy God is with thee whithersoever thou goest.—Joshua i, 9.

Fear not, but let your hands be strong.—Zech. viii, 13.

14. Ye are My witnesses that I am God.—Isa. xliii, 12.

Who is on the Lord's side?—Exod. xxxii, 26.

15. Wash *from sin*, purify, put away the evil of your doings from before Mine eyes; cease to do evil.—Isa. i, 16.

Learn to do well; seek judgment; relieve the oppressed, judge the fatherless, plead for the widow.—Isa. i, 17.

16. I acknowledged my sin unto Thee and mine iniquity have I not hid.—I said I will confess my transgressions unto the Lord, and Thou forgavest the iniquity of my sin.—Psalm xxxii, 5.

Seek ye Me, and live.—Amos v, 4.

Blessed is the man that walketh not in the counsel of the ungodly, nor standeth in the way of sinners, nor sitteth in the seat of the scornful.—Psalm i, 1.

A just man may fall seven times but he riseth up again.—Prov. xxiv, 16.

He hath shown thee, O man, what is good. And what doth the Lord require of thee, but to do justly, and to love mercy, and to walk humbly with thy God?—Micah vi, 8.

These are the things that ye shall do; speak ye everyone the truth to his neighbor; execute the judgment of truth and peace in your gates.—Zech. viii, 16.

Let no one of you imagine evil in your hearts against his neighbor; and love no false oath: for these are things that I hate, saith the Lord.—Zech. viii, 17.

17. Ye shall not seek after your hearts and your eyes after which ye go astray.—Numbers xv, 39.

HOLY DAYS AND FESTIVALS

12

THE SABBATH.

1. There are six "Assemblies of the Lord," or Holy Convocations. They are usually called Holydays or Festivals.

2. They are the Sabbath, the New Year and the Day of Atonement, which are called Holydays, and Passover, Pentecost and Tabernacles, which are called Festivals.

3. Holy Days and Festivals are days on which we are to assemble for the worship of God and for instruction in holy duties.

4. All work is forbidden upon those days.

5. Amusements which fatigue the body or the mind, or which are not in keeping with the holiness of the day, must be avoided.

THE SABBATH.

1. The Sabbath begins every Friday evening and lasts until Saturday nightfall.

2. It is kept to remind us of creation and of our deliverance from Egypt.

3. When God created this earth, He stored it with everything necessary for our earthly wants: food, material for raiment, beautiful views, forms and colors. And He commanded work, because work is necessary for our happiness.

4. But man has other than earthly wants. The true man desires to know more and more about God and to learn more and more how to please Him. That is, man has spiritual wants besides material needs.

5. If we used every day for only our earthly pleasures, or to obtain only our earthly wants, we would never have the opportunity to learn about God.

6. God therefore instituted the Sabbath, first, to give us a regular day of rest

from our usual worldly work, and secondly, to give us a weekly opportunity for learning about Him and what He desires from us.

7. Therefore on the Sabbath we abstain from all work and devote part of the day to special worship in private, or with our families, or preferably in a synagogue or temple.

8. It is good to worship God and to learn about Him and how we can best please Him every day. And we must do so. But the Seventh Day is the Sabbath of the Lord. On that day we should seek special instruction in the knowledge of God, the Creator, from men able to give it.

*9. The Sabbath is named as the first of the "Assembly Days" commanded by the Lord, thus implying that we are to assemble on the Sabbath for sacred purposes.

10. On other days of the week we cannot so well assemble for public worship, because worldly duties, permitted on those days, prevent us.

11. The Sabbath also reminds us of the deliverance from Egypt. We were slaves there and the labor which we had to perform was rigorous. It was hard bondage. We can therefore appreciate a restful Sabbath.

12. We were delivered from Egypt in order to be ministers of God among mankind; that is, to teach mankind by our example, as well as by our Bible. Therefore, on the Sabbath we devote time to learn about God and Duty, and how to teach mankind the truths thereof. For this reason we should listen to sermons on that day and read the Bible or other religious literature.

13. On Sabbath Eve (Friday night), the mother lights the Sabbath Lights. These are usually two, but sometimes seven. The lighting of the lamps is a sign of joy, the joy of Sabbath family-union, the joy of Sabbath evenings at home. It is the mother who can best secure this joy and she can do so by praying that the Light of God's countenance may bless all her loved ones in her home, even as the father repeats these solemn words, when on the Sabbath Eve, he blesses his children with the blessing of God for Israel.

14. Besides blessing the children on Sabbath Eve, the father, or head of the family, pronounces the Sabbath sanctification before the evening meal (see prayer book), and he or one of the family should say aloud "grace" or "blessing" after it.

15. On the Sabbath Day we should make every effort to attend public worship.

16. In some synagogues and homes the close of Sabbath is marked by the Havdalah, or "Division Ceremony," so called because it divides the Sabbath from the working days.

17. The object of the ceremony is to consecrate our five senses which will be used during the coming working days, and to bless God for our possession of each of them. Hence we pronounce a blessing over wine or something to *taste;* we *smell* the spices; we *feel* the heat of the light; we *see* these things, and we *hear* the words of benediction. Other explanations are also given.

18. We therefore begin and end the Sabbath just as we keep the whole day

itself—we make it "a sign" of the relations between God and ourselves, that we may "know that He is the Lord who consecrates us."

19. "It (the Sabbath) is holy for you" (Exod. xxxi. 14) means also that it consecrates Israel. For whoever observes the Sabbath testifies thereby to Creation and the Creator. He becomes a "witness for God" (Isa. xliii. 10), and is therefore consecrated to His service. See chapter xi. 9-16.

BIBLE QUOTATIONS.

1. Speak unto the children of Israel, and tell them the assemblies of the Lord, which ye shall proclaim *to be* holy Convocations, these are they, My assemblies.—Levit. xxiii, 2.

3. These are the assemblies of the Lord, even holy convocations, which ye shall proclaim in their seasons.—Levit. xxiii, 4.

4. Ye shall do no work thereon.—Levit. xxiii, 3, 7, 21, 27, 28, 31, 36.

THE SABBATH.

2. For in six days the Lord made heaven and earth, the sea and all that in them is, and He ceased on the seventh day. Therefore the Lord blessed the Sabbath Day and hallowed it.—Exod. xx, 11.

Remember that thou wast a servant in the land of Egypt, and that the Lord thy God brought thee out thence through a mighty hand and a stretched-out arm; therefore the Lord thy God commanded thee to keep the Sabbath Day.—Deut. v, 15.

3. And the Lord God took man and put him in the Garden of Eden to cultivate it and take care of it.—Gen. ii, 15.

Six days shalt thou labor and do all thy work.—Exod. xx, 9.

4. My soul thirsteth for God, for the living God; when shall I come and appear before God?—Psalm xlii, 2.

6. Six days shalt thou do thy work, and on the seventh day thou shalt rest; that thine ox and thine ass may rest and that the son of thy handmaid, and the stranger may be refreshed.

The seventh day is the Sabbath of the Lord thy God.—Exod. xx, 10.

7. And it shall come to pass, that from one new moon to another, and from one Sabbath to another, shall all flesh come to worship before Me, saith the Lord.—Isa. lxvi, 23.

13. The blessing of Israel, or Jacob, our ancestor, is:

May God make thee like Ephraim and Manasseh.—Gen. xlviii, 20.

The blessing for Israel, our people, is:

May the Lord bless thee and preserve thee;
May the Lord cause His countenance to shine upon thee and be
    gracious unto thee;

May the Lord lift up His countenance upon thee and grant thee peace.—Numbers vi, 24-26.

14. Verily My Sabbaths ye shall keep; for it is a sign between Me and you throughout your generations, that ye may know that I am the Lord who doth sanctify you.—Exod. xxxi, 13.

18. And the children of Israel shall keep the Sabbath, to observe the Sabbath throughout their generations, for a perpetual covenant. Between Me and the children of Israel it is a sign for ever.—Exod. xxxi, 16-17.

13

NEW YEAR (ROSH HASHANA)

1. The New Year is called in Hebrew Rosh Hashana.
2. It is kept in memory of the creation of the heavens and the earth.
3. When we behold the heavens with the countless stars or worlds immensely larger than the earth upon which we live, and remember that it was God who created them, and that it is He who governs them, we are filled with reverence for Him.
4. When we learn about the earth and find how God has stored it with everything necessary for our happiness, we cannot but love Him.
5. On each New Year we should resolve to prove by our conduct that we do reverence and love Him.
*6. On the New Year Holyday we prepare to meet our God.
7. We do this by examining our conduct during the past year, and by firmly resolving to correct it wherever it has been wrong.
8. When we have removed our sins from us by sincere repentance and by sincere promise of amendment, then we may confidently approach God in prayer, or "meet Him," on the coming Day of Atonement.
9. The ten days from the New Year to the Day of Atonement are called "the Ten Days of Penitence."
10. Our life during these days should be more serious. We must repair any wrong we have committed, and remove any cause of ill-feeling between others and ourselves. A father cannot be pleased when his children are at variance. We are all children of our Father in Heaven.
11. Rosh Hashana is not a festival. Therefore it is not observed with festivities. It is one of the Holy Days, or "Days of Awe" (Yamim Noraim).
12. It is sometimes called "Day of Judgment" (Yom Hadin).

13. Because on that day we represent ourselves as being judged by God for our past lives.

14. It is also called "The Day of Sounding the Shofar," or ram's horn.

15. Because the Shofar is sounded on that day, to remind us to appear before the Lord.

16. It is the beginning of the Jewish civil New Year.

(For the Ecclesiastical New Year, New Year for Trees, etc., see Appendix IV.)

BIBLE QUOTATIONS.

3. The Heavens declare the glory of God and the firmament sheweth His handiwork.—Psalm xix, 1.

4. O Lord, how manifold are Thy works! in wisdom hast Thou made them all; the earth is full of Thy possessions.—Psalm civ, 24.

5. Reverence the Lord, ye His holy ones.—Psalm xxxiv, 9.

I love the Lord.—Psalm cxvi, 1.

6. Prepare to meet thy God, O Israel.—Amos iv, 12.

7. Sow to yourselves in righteousness, reap in mercy; break up your fallow-ground; for it is time to seek the Lord, till He come and rain righteousness upon you.—Hoshea x, 12.

8. I will wash mine hands in innocence; so will I compass Thine altar, O Lord.—Psalm xxvi, 6.

10. If iniquity be in thine hand, put it far away, and let not wickedness dwell in thy tabernacles.—Job xi, 14.

13. For He cometh to judge the earth; with righteousness shall He judge the world and peoples with equity.—Psalm xcviii, 9.

14. And in the seventh month, on the first day of the month, ye shall have a holy convocation; ye shall do no servile work; it is a day of sounding *the shofar* unto you.—Numbers xxix, 1.

14

THE DAY OF ATONEMENT (KIPPUR)

1. The Day of Atonement is called in Hebrew Yom Kippur.
2. It is the day on which we solemnly ask pardon from God for sins which we have committed against Him.
3. Pardon is granted to us for those sins only when God, who knows our hearts, sees that our repentence is sincere.
4. On Yom Kippur we do not obtain pardon for sins committed against our fellow-being unless we have righted any wrong we have done to him.
5. We fast on the Day of Atonement.
6. We fast in order to humble ourselves before God, to realize how dependent we are upon Him for food, and therefore for life, and to learn to restrain earthly desires.
*7. "Fasting" in Hebrew is called "afflicting the soul."
8. We must be conscious of deep remorse for having offended God in the past year by any wrong-doing to Him or to our neighbor by word, deed or thought, and must make a sincere confession of our faults.
9. Remorse, or real sorrow for sin committed, is the beginning of repentance. To be complete, it must be followed by amendment of our conduct.
10. We pray for pardon for ourselves and for all Israel. Hence our confession includes sins which others have committed.
11. Atoning to God for our sins by offering to Him our contrite heart and sincere promise of amendment, makes us "at one" with Him. This "at-onement," or being "at one" with God, is the source of consolation and strength to the truly religious man or woman at all times.
12. Our sins separate us from God.
13. To be separated through our own fault from those whom we love, is always a source of deep sorrow, and we try to become reconciled. How much

greater should be our sorrow when our faults separate us from God, and how much more should we try to be at one with Him again!

14. God invites us to repent. He promises pardon if we do. He declares that He delights in pardoning the penitent.

BIBLE QUOTATIONS.

2. For on this day he shall make an atonement for you to cleanse you from all your sins; before the Lord ye shall be cleansed.—Levit. xvi, 30.

3. I, the Lord, search the heart; I try the reins, even to give every man according to his ways and according to the fruit of his doings.—Jerem. xvii, 10.

4. If a soul sin . . . then it shall be, because he hath sinned and is guilty, that he shall restore that which he robbed or that which he hath deceitfully gotten, or that which was confided to him, or the lost thing which he hath found, or all that about which he hath sworn falsely; he shall even restore it in the principal and shall add the fifth part thereto, and give it to him to whom it belongeth, in the day of his trespass-offering.—Levit. vi, 2-5.

5. And ye shall have on the tenth day of this seventh month a holy convocation; and ye shall afflict your souls; ye shall not do any work thereon.—Numbers xxix, 7.

7. Is it such a fast that I have chosen, a day for a man to afflict his soul?—Isa. lviii, 5.

8. The Lord is nigh unto them that are of a broken heart, and saveth such as be of a contrite spirit.—Psalm xxxiv, 17.

I acknowledged my sin unto Thee, and mine iniquity have I not hid. I said I will confess mine transgressions unto the Lord, and Thou forgavest the iniquity of my sin.—Psalm xxxii, 5.

Have mercy upon me, O God, according to Thy loving kindness; according to the multitude of Thy tender mercies, blot out my transgressions.—Psalm li. 1.

Wash me thoroughly from mine iniquity, and cleanse me from my sin.—Psalm li, 2.

For I acknowledge my transgressions, and my sin is ever before me.—Psalm li, 3.

9. The sacrifices of God are a broken spirit; a broken and a contrite heart, O God, Thou wilt not despise.—Psalm li, 17.

Create in me a clean heart, O God, and renew a right spirit within me.—Psalm li, 10.

Cast me not away from Thy presence, and take not Thy Holy Spirit from me.—Psalm li, 11.

10. And Moses returned to the Lord and said, O this people have sinned a great sin . . . . And now, if Thou wilt forgive their sin.—Exod. xxxii, 31-32.

Pardon, I beseech Thee, the iniquity of this people, according to the greatness of Thy mercy, and as Thou hast forgiven this people, from Egypt and even until now.—Numbers xiv, 19.

God be merciful unto us.—Psalm lxvii, 1.

11. Happy is he whose transgression is forgiven, whose sin is covered.—Psalm xxxii, 1.

Happy is the man unto whom the Lord imputeth not iniquity, and in whose spirit there is no guile.—Psalm xxxii, 2.

Thou, O Lord, hast helped me and consoled me.—Psalm lxxxvi, 17.

I lift mine eyes unto the mountains, whence cometh my help?—Psalm cxxi, 1.

My help is from the Lord who made heaven and earth.—Psalm cxxi, 2.

Let the wicked forsake his way and the man of iniquity his thoughts; and let him return unto the Lord, and He will have mercy upon him; and to our God, for He will abundantly pardon.—Isa. lv, 7.

12. Your iniquities separate between you and your God, and your sins hide His face from you, that He will not hear.—Isa. lix, 2.

Your sins withhold good from you.—Jerem. v, 25.

13. O God, Thou art my God; early will I seek Thee; my soul thirsteth for Thee; my whole being longeth for Thee.—Psalm lxiii, i.

14. If the wicked will turn from all his sins that he hath committed, and keep all My statutes, and do that which is lawful and right, he shall surely live, he shall not die.—Ezek. xviii, 21.

All his transgressions that he hath committed, they shall not be mentioned unto him; in his righteousness that he doeth, he shall live.—Ezek. xviii, 22.

Have I any pleasure at all that the wicked should die? saith the Lord God, and not that he should turn from his ways, and live?—Ezek. xviii, 23.

15

THE THREE FESTIVALS

The Passover or Pesach.

1. The Passover Festival is called in Hebrew, Pesach.

2. It is kept in honor of our Freedom, when we were delivered by God from Egypt, where our ancestors were slaves. (A. M. 2448.)

3. We may not eat or drink anything leavened or fermented during the whole Passover week.

4. The Hagada, or story of the departure from Egypt, is read in the home. The ceremony is called the Seder.

5. During the reading, the following symbols are used—a small piece of lamb bone, unleavened bread and bitter herb, a roasted egg and Haroseth.

6. The lamb bone is to remind us of the Pascal or Passover sacrifice offered by our ancestors on the night of the departure from Egypt, when they ate of the lamb, with unleavened bread and bitter herbs, after sprinkling the blood of the lamb on their door-posts.

7. The marking of the door-post with the blood was to prove that they believed in God and not in the gods of the Egyptians, such as the lamb.

8. The unleavened bread reminds us of God's love in ordering our fathers to get ready the only kind of bread that would be fit for their long journey from Egypt.

9. The bitter herb reminds us of the bitter bondage our fathers had to endure in Egypt.

10. When we contrast our freedom with their bondage we cannot but be grateful to God for His kindness and protection.

11. The great lessons of the Passover are therefore Faith in God, His love for us, our gratitude to Him.

*12. The roasted egg is a reminder of the "Festival Sacrifice," or the ancient national gathering of our fathers every Passover in Jerusalem.

13. The Haroseth represents the bricks and mortar with which our fathers labored in Egypt, and thus indicates the menial nature of their work.

14. Work is permitted on the middle days of Passover.

15. The importance of the Passover is shown by the frequency with which the deliverance from Egypt is mentioned in the Bible as the reason for many commands concerning our duty to God, to our neighbor and to ourselves.

16. And its importance is strikingly shown by the fact that the deliverance from Egypt is mentioned in the first of the ten commandments.

17. From the history of the Passover we learn these additional lessons:

1. Freedom is mankind's right.
2. No nation has any right to oppress another.
3. God judges every nation.
4. No nation can allow wrong in its midst without suffering for it.

BIBLE QUOTATIONS.

2. Remember this day, in which ye came out of Egypt, out of the house of bondage.—Exod. xiii, 3.

The feast of unleavened bread shalt thou keep. Seven days shalt thou eat unleavened bread, as I commanded thee, in the time of the month Abib; for in the month Abib thou camest out of Egypt.—Exod. xxxiv, 18.

3 Seven days shall there be no leaven found in your house.—Exod. xii, 19.

Ye shall eat nothing leavened.—Exod. xii, 20.

Unleavened bread shall be eaten seven days; and there shall no leavened bread be seen with thee, neither shall there be leaven seen with thee in all thy quarters.—Exod. xiii, 7.

4. And thou shalt tell thy son on that day, saying, this is done because of that which the Lord did for me when I came forth from Egypt.—Exod. xiii, 8.

5. And they shall eat the flesh on that night, roast with fire, and unleavened bread; and with bitter herbs shall they eat it.—Exod. xii, 8.

7. And against all the gods of Egypt I will execute judgments. I am the Lord.—Exod. xii, 12.

9. And they made their lives bitter with hard bondage in mortar and brick, and in all manner of service in the field; all their service, wherein they made them serve, was with rigor.—Exod. i, 14.

11. And the people had faith; and when they heard that the Lord had visited the children of Israel, and that He had looked upon their affliction, then they bowed their heads and worshiped.—Exod. iv, 31.

Because the Lord loved you and because He would keep the promise which He promised unto your fathers, hath the Lord brought you out with a mighty hand, and redeemed you out of the house of bondmen, from the hand of Pharaoh, King of Egypt.—Deut, vii, 8.

O give thanks unto the Lord, for He is good, for His mercy endureth for ever. Let the redeemed of the Lord say so, whom He hath redeemed from the hand of the enemy.—Psalm cvii, 1. 2.

12. At the place which the Lord thy God shall choose to place His name therein, there shalt thou sacrifice the Passover, at eventide, at the going down of the sun, at the season that thou camest forth out of Egypt.—Deut. xvi, 6.

13. And they embittered their lives with hard bondage in mortar and in brick.—Exod. i, 14.

14. And on the first day a holy convocation and on the seventh day a holy convocation shall there be to you; no manner of work shall be done on them, save that which everyone must eat, that only may be done for you.—Exod. xii, 16.

15. Ye shall keep My commandments and do them; I am the Lord. Ye shall not profane My Holy Name, but I will be hallowed among the children of Israel; I am the Lord who halloweth you, that brought you out of the land of Egypt, to be your God; I am the Lord your God.—Levit. xxii, 31-33.

If thy brother become poor and fall in need with thee, then thou shalt relieve him, yea though he be a stranger or a sojourner, that he may live with thee. Take thou no usury nor interest of him, but fear thy God . . . I am the Lord your God who brought you forth out of the land of Egypt.—Levit. xxv, 35-38.

Just balances, just weights, a just ephah and a just hin shall ye have. I am the Lord your God, who brought you out of the land of Egypt.—Levit. xix, 36.

Be ye holy to your God. I am the Lord your God who brought you out of the land of Egypt to be your God.—Numbers xv, 40-41.

17. Proclaim liberty throughout the land unto all the inhabitants thereof.—Lev. xxv, 10.

Thou shalt take up this proverb against the King of Babylon, and say, How hath the oppressor ceased!—Isa. xiv, 4.

With righteousness shall He judge the world and peoples with equity.—Psalm xcviii, 9.

If *a nation* do evil in My sight, that it obey not My voice, then I will reconsider the good, wherewith I said I would benefit them.—Jerem. xviii, 10.

16

THE SECOND FESTIVAL

Feast of Weeks or Shavuoth.

1. The Feast of Weeks is called in Hebrew, "Shavuoth."
2. It commemorates the giving of the ten commandments on Mt. Sinai. (A. M. 2448.)
3. When the ten commandments were given to us, God declared we were to be a kingdom of priests and a Holy nation.
4. To be a kingdom of priests means to teach what is right to all nations.
5. We do teach them by means of our Bible and by our own example.
6. In order to teach all nations we live in all parts of the world.
*7. To be a holy nation means that we are to live holy or pure lives.
8. God has consecrated us to be His servants or instruments on earth to lead mankind to righteousness. Therefore we must live righteously.
9. We are consecrated to God when we stand or witness for God and the Right.
10. To be "the kingdom of priests," "a consecrated nation," or "God's witnesses," is a great honor. It distinguishes us from all others.
11. But it is only for the praise, the name and the glory of God that we have been so selected.
12. Our responsibilities are all the greater. For it is especially our duty always to set the right example.
13. This Festival has the following names.

"Day of Giving the Law," because the Law was given thereon.
"Pentecost," meaning fifty, because it is the fiftieth day after Passover
    begins.

"Feast of Harvest," because it is the season of wheat harvest.

"Day of first fruits," because our fathers in Palestine used to take an offering of the first fruits in gratitude to God.

14. The days between the first day of Passover and the first day of the Feast of Weeks are called "Days of the Omer."

15. The Omer was an ancient Hebrew measure.

16. Our ancestors used to offer an omer of barley on the second day of Passover, and seven weeks or forty-nine days were then counted to the Feast of Weeks.

17. To-day we count the days. It is called "Counting the Omer."

18. It has become a period of sadness, owing to certain later and sad events in our history. (See *Appendix V.*)

BIBLE QUOTATIONS.

2. In the third month, when the children of Israel were gone forth out of the land of Egypt, the same day came they into the wilderness of Sinai.—Exod. xix, 1.

3. And ye shall be unto Me a kingdom of priests and a holy nation—Exod. xix, 6.

4. This people have I formed for Myself, they shall declare My praise.—Isa. xliii, 21.

Ye shall be named the Priests of the Lord; men shall call you the Ministers of our God.—Isa. lxi, 6.

5. And He said unto me, thou art My servant, O Israel, by whom I will be glorified . . . . I will also appoint thee for a light to the Gentiles, that thou mayst be My salvation unto the ends of the earth.—Isa. xlix, 3-6.

To make known to mankind His mighty acts and the glorious majesty of His kingdom.—Psalm cxlv, 12.

6. Israel shall blossom and bud, and fill the face of the world with fruit.—Isa. xxvii, 6.

8. Thou art My servant; I have found thee; thou art My servant.—Isa. xliv, 21.

Behold My servant whom I uphold; Mine elect in whom my soul delighteth. I have put My Spirit upon him; he shall bring forth judgment to the Gentiles.—Isa. xlii, 1.

He shall not fail nor be discouraged, till he have set judgment in the earth; and the isles shall wait for his law.—Isa. xlii, 4.

I, the Lord, have called thee in righteousness, and will hold thine hand and will keep thee, and will give thee for a covenant of the peoples, for a light of the Gentiles.—Isa. xlii, 6.

To open eyes that are blind, to bring out prisoners from the prison and them that sit in darkness out of the prison house.—Isa. xlii, 7.

10. And now, if ye will obey My voice, indeed, and keep My covenant, then ye shall be to Me a peculiar treasure above all the peoples.—Exod. xix, 5.

11. And to make thee high above all nations which He hath made, for praise and for a name and for honor; and that thou mayst be a holy people unto the Lord thy God, as He hath spoken.—Deut. xxvi, 18-19.

13. Until the morrow after the seventh week ye shall count fifty days, and ye shall bring a new oblation to the Lord. . . . first fruits to the Lord.—Levit. xxiii, 16, 17.

And thou shalt observe the feast of weeks of the first fruits of wheat harvest.—Exod. xxxiv, 22.

And on the day of first fruits, when ye offer a new oblation to the Lord, on your feast of weeks, ye shall have a holy convocation. Ye shall not do any servile work.—Numbers xxviii, 26.

17. And ye shall count unto you from the morrow after the Sabbath, from the day that ye brought the sheaf of the wave-offering; seven Sabbaths shall be complete.

17

SUCCOTH, OR THE FESTIVAL OF TABERNACLES

1. The third festival is called Tabernacles, in Hebrew Succoth.

2. It is kept to remind us of God's loving protection of our fathers when He caused them to be sheltered in booths or tabernacles in their journey through the deserts, after they left Egypt.

3. In warm climates we live in a tabernacle for the whole week.

4. In colder climates we enter a tabernacle and bless God therein.

5. In our synagogues, a palm-branch, a citron, some myrtle, and willow are used during service.

*6. The palm-branch (lulab) represents our frame; the citron (ethrog) represents the heart; the myrtle-leaf (hadas) represents the eye, and the willow-leaf (arbe nahal) represents the lips, teaching thus that our frame, our heart, our eyes, and our lips are to be used in the service of God.

7. The seventh day of the festival is called "Hosana Rabba," the great salvation, when a last appeal is made for God's saving grace and pardon.

8. The eighth day is called "The Eighth Day of Solemn Assembly." In our synagogues a prayer is offered asking God to send rain in its season, so that earth may produce bountiful harvests next year.

9. The festival is sometimes called "the Feast of Ingathering," because it ended the season of "gathering in" the grape and other fruit harvests.

10. It closes the year's great festivals. At the end of each year it is well for us to think of what we have gathered in, or what we might have gathered in—the blessings of God, the love of our parents, the good will of our teachers, the respect of all who know us.

11. The following day is called Simhat Torah, or Rejoicing of the Law.

12. Because the reading of the Law, or Torah, is ended and recommenced every year on that day.

13. Two gentlemen are honored by being called to the Law, one when the last chapter is read, and one when the first chapter is recommenced.

14. The former is called the Bridegroom of the Law (Hatan Torah); the latter is called the Bridegroom of the Beginning (Hatan Bereshith).

15. Work is permitted on the middle days of Tabernacles.

Table of the Dates of the Holydays and Festivals.
HOLYDAYS.

1. Sabbath—From Friday sunset to Saturday nightfall, every week.
2. New Year, or Rosh Hashana

1st Tishri.[a]

3. Day of Atonement, or Kippur

10th Tishri.

FESTIVALS.

1. Passover, or Pesach

15th Nissan[a]

(7th Day of Passover

21st Nissan[a])

2. Feast of Weeks, or Shavuoth

6th Sivan[a]

3. Tabernacles, or Succoth

15th Tishri[a]

Eighth Day of Solemn Assembly

22nd Tishri[b]

The "second day Holyday," as it is called, was orally instituted through doubt as to the correct day to be observed. Orthodox Hebrews hold that it must be observed until abrogated by authority of a body of qualified Rabbis.

[a] The following day is also observed by orthodox Hebrews. [b] The day following is Simhat Torah, or Rejoicing of the Law. (See *Chap. xvii. No. 11.*)

BIBLE QUOTATIONS.

1. The fifteenth day of this seventh month shall be the feast of the Tabernacles for seven days unto the Lord.—Levit. xxiii, 34.

2. Ye shall dwell in booths seven days, every Israelite-born shall dwell in booths. That your generations may know that I made the children of Israel to dwell in booths when I brought them out of the land of Egypt.—Levit. xxiii, 43.

5. And ye shall take for yourselves on the first day the boughs of goodly trees, branches of palm trees, and the boughs of thick trees and willows of the brook; and ye shall rejoice before the Lord seven days.—Levit. xxiii, 40.

8. On the eighth day shall be a holy convocation to you . . . it is a solemn assembly; and ye shall do no servile work thereon.—Levit. xxiii, 36.

9. And thou shalt observe the feast of ingathering at the year's end.—Exod. xxxiv, 22.

THE MINOR FESTIVALS.

18

HANUKAH.

1. There are two minor festivals, or festivals not commanded to us by Moses.

2. These are the Feast of Dedication (Hanukah), and Feast of Lots (Purim).

3. We are permitted to work on both.

4. Hanukah is kept in memory of the successful resistance of the Jews, under Judas Maccabeus, against the Syrians and Greeks under Antiochus, who tried to destroy our religion.

5. The festival lasts for eight days, in memory of the eight days that were used by Judas to cleanse the Temple (165 B. C. E.) after its defilement by the Syrians and Greeks. It begins on the 25th of Kislev.

6. We light lamps each night in memory of the oil for the Temple lamps found by Judas, and which was enough to last until more could be made.

*7. The fight of the Jews, or Maccabees (followers of Judas Maccabeus) as they were called, was really a fight between Monotheism or belief in One God, and of Paganism or Polytheism, the belief in many gods.

8. If Antiochus had defeated Judas, Monotheism, or our religion would have been destroyed, Christianity and Mohammedanism would have been impossible, and modern civilization would have been replaced by pagan immorality.

9. The story of Hanukah tells us of many heroes and heroines, marytrs for God and our religion, men and women as brave and as noble as any in the history of any country.

APOCRYPHA QUOTATIONS.

Moreover King Antiochus wrote to his whole kingdom, that all should be one people, and everyone should leave his laws.—1 Maccabees i, 41, 42.

For the king sent letters by messengers unto Jerusalem and the cities of Juda, that they should follow the strange laws of the land.

And forbid offerings . . . and profane the sabbaths and festival days, and pollute the sanctuary and holy people . . . set up altars and groves, and chapels of idols, and sacrifice swine's flesh, and unclean beasts. . . .

To the end that they might forget the law. . . .

And whosoever would not do according to the commandment of the King, should die.—44-50.

Then Judas, called Maccabeus, rose up . . . salvation prospered in his hand. —Chap. iii, 1, 6.

Then said Judas and his brethren, behold our enemies are discomfited: let us go up to cleanse and dedicate the sanctuary.—Chap. iv, 36.

And they kept the dedication of the altar eight days . . . Moreover Judas and his brethren with the whole congregation of Israel ordained that the days of the dedication of the altar should be kept in their season from year to year by the space of eight days, from the five and twentieth day of the month Kislev, with mirth and gladness—v, 59.

19

PURIM

1. Purim is kept on the 14th and 15th Adar in memory of the deliverance of the Jews of Persia from their destruction. (A. M. 3404.)

2. Haman, prime-minister of Ahasveros, King of Persia, obtained permission to destroy all the Jews. He cast lots, in order to find what he thought would be a lucky day for their massacre. He chose the 14th Adar.

3. Hence the festival is called the "Feast of Lots" or "Purim."

4. But Mordechai, a Jew, cousin of Esther, the queen, sent word to her to try and save her people.

5. She succeeded, and with Mordechai, commanded all Jews to observe the 14th and 15th of Adar as a festival.

6. We celebrate the festival by rejoicing and by gifts to the poor.

7. We have always had brave men and women to encourage and defend us in the face of danger. Courage to defend our race and religion distinguishes every true-hearted Jew and Jewess.

BIBLE QUOTATIONS.

2. Because Haman, the son of Hammedatha, the Agagite, the enemy of all the Jews, had devised against the Jews to destroy them, and had cast Pur, that is, the lot, to consume them and to destroy them.—Esther ix, 24.

But when Esther came before the King, he commanded by letter that his wicked device, which he devised against the Jews, should return upon his own head, and that he and his sons should be hanged on the gallows.—Esther ix, 25.

5. And Mordecai sent letters to all the Jews that were in the provinces of the King Ahasveros, both nigh and far, to establish among them that they should

keep the fourteenth of Adar and the fifteenth day of the same, yearly.—Esther ix, 20-21.

Then Esther the queen, the daughter of Abihail, and Mordecai the Jew, wrote with all authority, to confirm.—Esther ix, 29.

6. And Mordecai wrote . . . . that they should make them days of feasting and of joy, and of sending portions one to another, and gifts to the poor.—Esther ix. 20-22.

20

THE MINOR FASTS

*1. There are six minor fasts observed as follows:

NAME: Tamuz
DATE: 17th of Tamuz.
REASON: Capture of Jerusalem and siege of the second Temple by the Romans under Titus, 3828 A. M.

NAME: Ab
DATE: 9th of Ab.
REASON: Capture of the first Temple by Nebuchadnezzar, King of Babylon, 3338 A. M., and of the second Temple, by Titus, general of the Romans, 3828 A. M.

NAME: Guedalia
DATE: 3rd Tishri.
REASON: Murder of Guedalia, governor of the Jews appointed by Nebuchadnezzar and consequent sufferings of the Jews left in Palestine.

NAME: Tebet
DATE: 10 Tebet.
REASON: Siege of the city and first temple begun by Nebuchadnezzar.

NAME: Esther
DATE: 13 Adar.
REASON: In memory of the fast of Queen Esther of Persia before she went before King Ahasveros to save her people, the Jews.

NAME: Fast of the first-born
DATE: 14 Nissan.
REASON: Observed only by first-born (sons) in memory of the death of all the first-born of Egypt at the exodus of the Hebrews.

THE TEN COMMANDMENTS.

21

THE FIRST COMMANDMENT.

*1. The Ten Commandments are the most important Commands of God and include all others. They were given to the Hebrews on Mt. Sinai, about two months after they left Egypt, A. M. 2448.

2. The Ten Commandments are called in Hebrew "Asereth Hadebarim"—"the ten words or declarations." In English they are called "the decalogue," from two Greek words, *deka* ten, *logoi*, words.

3. Our sages love to point out that the Commandments were given on a low mountain, Sinai, and not on a towering height, like Lebanon, etc., teaching us that the knowledge of the law is best when united with humility. They further bid us observe that the Law was given not in Palestine, the land of Israel, lest Israel should ever say the law was meant for him alone. It was given in the wilderness which is open to all, thus to teach us that the law is for all mankind.

THE FIRST COMMANDMENT.

**I am the Lord thy God who hath brought thee forth
from the land of Egypt, out of the house of bondage.**

1. From this we learn

>   1st. There is a God. He is the Lord.
>   2ndly. He is our God.
>   3rdly. It was He who delivered us from Egypt.

2. We know there is a God from what the Bible tells us and from Nature.

3. The Bible contains His messages to mankind, through men and women worthy to convey them.

4. Nature tells us there is a God by the wonders of the Heavens and the Earth and the laws that govern them.

5. Our knowledge of God leads us to Reverence and Love for Him.

6. Since we owe to Him our rescue from Egypt, we cannot be sufficiently grateful to Him.

7. Our gratitude is best proved by our obedience to His commands.

*8. That He is our God is one of the fundamentals of our religion. It was first announced to the patriarchs in what is called the Bircath Abraham, or Blessing of Abraham, and is constantly referred to by the prophets.

9. The Bircath Abraham was thus repeated to Jacob: "I am the Lord God of Abraham thy father, and the God of Isaac, the land whereon thou liest to thee will I give it, and to thy seed. And thy seed shall be as the dust of the earth, and thou shalt spread abroad to the west, and to the east, and to the north and to the south; and in thee and in thy seed shall all the families of the earth be blessed." (Gen. xxviii, 13-14.)

10. It contains therefore, four declarations:

1. He is our God.
2. Palestine has been given by Him to us.
3. We are to be found also throughout the world.
4. We are to be a source of blessing to mankind.

11. We are to teach all mankind to recognize Him as their one God also.

12. The possession of Palestine and our dispersion throughout the world are for mankind's benefit. (See xlii, 13 to end of chapter). Hence, when we possessed Palestine and King Solomon dedicated the Temple, that crowning glory of the nation and the embodiment of its mission of the earth, he declared it to be "In order that all the peoples of the earth may know that the Lord, He is the God, there is none other." I Kings viii, 60.

13. We have been a blessing to the nations of the earth in our dispersion among them, by our having carried to them the Bible, the Book of Books, mankind's greatest blessing and priceless possession. We preserved for mankind the knowledge of God through the pagan, the dark and the middle ages. Our ten Commandments are recognized as fundamental among all civilized nations. The wisdom of our Torah is recognized universally. The ideals of our Bible are the ideals of humanity. And our psalms are read and sung in worship in countless cathedrals and churches, while they comfort and inspire countless hearts and homes.

14. We will continue to be a source of "blessing to all the families of the earth" in our continued dispersion among them, by showing through the lives we lead, the wisdom and beauty of our Torah, and the ethical value of our religion and its ceremonies; by our loyalty to the ideals of our Bible, and by our

standing at all times for God and the Right. When Jewish life means honor, when Jewish homes mean love, and when Jewish citizenship means righteousness, then Jewish example becomes a source of blessing to "all the families of earth."

15. We will be a source of blessing to all mankind when Zion or Palestine becomes the spiritual center for all the world, a spiritual influence to quicken man's sense of duty to God and humanity. Nations will carry thither their disputes for adjudication. Hence war and its curses will be abolished. Through its influence earth will be filled with the knowledge of the Lord as the waters cover the sea. All nations will gradually learn that the Lord is God, the only God, and King over all the earth.

16. The Bircath Abraham, given first to Abraham, the founder of the ancient Hebrew nation, therefore contains in it the ideal of the universal kingdom of God. To Him, the El Olam, Abraham built the first altar, and of Him all our prophets preached, from Moses to Malachi.

BIBLE QUOTATIONS.

2. And he wrote upon the tablets the words of the covenant, the ten declarations.—Exod. xxxiv, 28.

THE FIRST COMMANDMENT

2. The Lord, He is the God.—I Kings xviii, 39.
3. Hear ye the word of the Lord.—Jer. ii, 4.
4. Lo these *wonders of nature* are but whispers of His ways; but how little a portion is heard of Him! Then the thunder of His power, who can understand?—Job xxvi, 14.
10. —

(1) He is thy God.—Deut. x, 21.
(2) I made the earth . . . . and I give it unto whom it seemeth meet unto Me.—Jerem. xxvii, 5.
And I will give unto thee and to thy seed after thee, the land of thy sojournings, all the land of Canaan for an everlasting possession.—Gen. xvii, 8.
(3) And thy seed shall be known among the nations and their offspring among the peoples.—Isa. lxi, 9.
And I will sow them among the peoples; and they shall remember Me in far countries.—Zach. x, 9.
(4) Israel shall blossom and bud and shall fill the face of the world with fruit.—Isa. xxvii, 6.
And in thy seed shall all the nations of the earth be blessed.—Gen. xxii, 18; xxvi, 4.

11. I, the Lord, have called thee in righteousness . . . . I give thee for a light for the nations.—Isa. xlii, 6.

To make known to mankind His mighty acts and the glorious majesty of His kingdom.—Psalm cxlv, 12.

God, the God of all mankind.

God, God, of the Spirits of all Flesh.—Numbers xvi, 22; xxvii, 16.

Yea, He loveth peoples.—Deut. xxxiii, 3.

My house shall be called a house of prayer for all the peoples.—Isa. lvi, 7.

And it shall come to pass in the last days, that the mountain of the Lord's house shall be established . . . . and all nations shall flow into it.—Isa ii, 2, and Micah iv, 1.

12. And the remnant of Jacob shall be in the midst of many peoples as a dew from the Lord, as the showers upon the grass.—Micah v, 6.

14. Israel is My son, my first-born.—Exod. iv, 22.

Remember these things, O Jacob, O Israel; for thou art My servant. I have formed thee, thou art My servant.—Isa. xliv, 21.

Thou art My servant, O Israel, by whom I will be glorified . . . . I will give thee for a light to the Gentiles, that thou mayst be My salvation to the end of the earth.—Isa. xlix, 3-6.

Thus saith the Lord . . . . I will preserve thee and give thee for a covenant of the peoples, to establish the earth.—Isa. xlix, 8.

15. Out of Zion shall go forth law and the word of the Lord from Jerusalem. —Isa. ii, 3; Micah iv, 2.

And He shall judge among the nations and shall rebuke many peoples.— Isa. ii, 4; cf. Micah iv, 3.

They shall beat their swords into plowshares and their spears into pruning hooks; nation shall not lift up sword against nation; neither shall they learn war any more.—Isa. ii, 4; Micah iv, 3.

Earth shall be filled with the knowledge of the glory of the Lord as the waters cover the sea.—Hab. ii. 14.

And the Lord will be king over all the earth, in that day the Lord will be one and His Name One.—Zech. xiv, 9. (See also chapter xvi. Quotations 3-9.)

16. And Abraham proclaimed there by the name of the Lord, the God of the universe.—Gen. xxi, 33.

All the earth shall be filled with the glory of the Lord.—Numbers xiv, 20.

Have we not all one Father?—Malachi ii, 10.

22

THE SECOND COMMANDMENT

1. Thou shalt not have any other gods before Me.
* Thou shalt not make unto thyself any graven image or any likeness of anything that is in the heavens above, or that is on the earth beneath or that is in the waters under the earth.

Thou shalt not bow down thyself to them nor serve them, for I, the Lord thy God, am a zealous God, visiting the iniquity of fathers upon children of the third and fourth generations of those that hate Me,

And showing loving-kindness unto the thousands of those that love Me and keep My Commandments.

2. This commandment teaches us that there is only one God.

3. He is our God and we do not believe that there are any other gods.

4. Therefore to worship any being except the one and only God, is a sin. It is called idolatry.

5. Self-Conceit, to give way to violent outbursts of passion, etc., are declared by our sages to be tantamount to idolatry. For the former shows that self, and the latter that passion, is a greater power with us than God is.

6. God often delays the punishment of our sins so as to give us every chance to repent, just as He says in this commandment, that He waits to the third and fourth generation.

7. If we believe in the one true God, we can prove it by not neglecting or disobeying Him for the sake of anything.

Many neglect Him for the sake of business, or pleasure, which is as much as saying that business or pleasure is a greater power than God.

8. "Visiting the iniquity of fathers upon children of the third and fourth generation of those that hate Me" teaches that immorality of parents transmits

its terrible results to children of the third or fourth generation. Idolatry in ancient days, always included immorality.

9. Our Bible declares that parents shall not suffer for the sins of their children, nor children for sins of parents.

10. This means that the punishment for every sin must be borne by the one who sins.

11. But though the penalty for a sin is to be inflicted only on the sinner, the shame and the loss are felt by one's family.

12. Moses asked God to be punished for the Israelites who had sinned by their idolatry of the golden calf. God told him that whoever sinned must suffer.

13. To suffer punishment for others' sins in order that the sinners may be pardoned, is called vicarious atonement. We Hebrews do not believe in it (See chapters xxxix, 8; xli, 11; Part II).

14. Our sages teach that no one can deny his friend, without denying his God, and no man goes to commit a wrong act without first denying Him who forbids it. Any disloyalty to God or denial of Him is equivalent to idolatry, for it shows that personal feeling is with us a greater power than God.

BIBLE QUOTATIONS.

Hear, O Israel, the Lord is our God, the Lord is One.—Deut. iv, 6.

3. He is our God.—Joshua xxiv, 18.

Now I know that there is no God in all the earth but in Israel.—II. Kings v, 15.

There is no God else beside Me; a just God and a Savior; there is none beside Me.—Isa. xlv, 21.

4. Thou shalt worship no other God.—Exod. xxxiv, 14.

5. When thou seest a man wise in his own eyes, then is there more hope for a fool than for him.—Prov. xxvi, 12.

Keep me from the violent man.—Ps. cxl, 1.

He that is soon angry commiteth folly.—Prov. xiv, 17.

9. The son shall not bear the iniquity of the father, neither shall the father bear the iniquity of the son.—Ezek. xviii, 20.

10. The soul that sinneth it shall die.—Ezek. xviii, 4.

12. Yet now, if Thou will forgive their sin—and if not, blot me out, I pray Thee.—Exod. xxxiii, 32.

And the Lord said unto Moses, whosoever hath sinned against Me, him will I blot out of My book.—Exod. xxxiii, 33.

23

THE THIRD COMMANDMENT

1. **Thou shalt not take the name of the Lord thy God in vain; for the Lord will not hold him guiltless that taketh His name in vain.**
2. We take His name in vain when we say it in any disrespectful way, for false oath or for any wrong purpose, or when we say our prayers, without thinking reverently of what we say.
3. We take His name in vain, or to no purpose, if we speak of God being good, just, merciful, etc., without trying ourselves to be good, just, merciful, etc. We therefore must show a loving nature, we must be merciful to others' faults, forbearing with their short-comings, and forgiving when we have been wronged. For He is merciful, forbearing and forgiving.
*4. We are children of God. We are called by His name. When we do wrong, we disgrace or profane His name. Hence a disgraceful act is called Chilul Hashem, a profanation of the Name.
5. And just as all the members of a family feel any disgrace that any one of them incurs, so when any Hebrew does wrong, the disgrace is felt by all Jews.
6. We are known as the people of God. We assume His name in vain unless we obey His Laws.
7. We take or assume His name in vain if we call ourselves Jews but live like heathens, without ever praying to God to acknowledge His power, to declare our needs, or to thank Him for His blessings.
8. We take or assume His name in vain if we call ourselves Jew's but adopt non-Jewish religious customs or observances.
9. We take or assume His name in vain if we speak of His goodness to all creatures and His laws of kindness to animals unless we also are good and kind to them.
10. We take or assume His name in vain when we call ourselves by His

name and say we are His children or His people, while for our convenience or ease we neglect religious duties which He has commanded us.

11. And we take or assume His name in vain, when we invent excuses to justify our neglect or disobedience of His Laws, as if our wisdom were greater than His.

BIBLE QUOTATIONS.

2. To reverence this glorious and awe-inspiring Name, the Lord thy God.--Deut. xxviii, 58.

Ye shall not swear by My Name falsely, neither shalt thou profane the name of thy God. I am the Lord.--Lev. xix, 12.

I will be sanctified by them that come nigh to Me.--Lev. x, 3.

Serve the Lord with reverence.--Psalm ii, 11.

3. Ye shall walk after the Lord your God, and reverence Him, and keep His commandments and obey His voice; and ye shall serve Him and cleave to Him.--Deut. xiii, 4.

4. Ye are the children of the Lord your God.--Deut. xiv, 1.

We are called by Thy name.--Jerem. xiv, 9.

Ye shall not profane My holy name, but I will be sanctified in the midst of the children of Israel. I am the Lord who halloweth you.--Lev. xxii, 32.

6. Thou art My people.--Isa. li. 16.

I will be their God and they shall be My people.--Ezek. xxxvii, 27.

7. Evening, morn and noon will I pray and cry aloud, and He will hear my voice.--Psalm lv, 17.

8. Take heed to thyself . . . . lest thou seek after their gods, saying, how do these nations serve their gods, I will do so likewise.--Deut. xii, 30.

9. A righteous man regardeth the life of his beast.--Prov. xii, 10.

10. A son honoreth his father and a servant his master. If then I be a Father where is Mine honor, and if I be a Master, where is My respect? saith the Lord of Hosts, unto you, O priests, that despise My name.--Mal. i, 6.

11. Woe unto them that are wise in their own eyes and prudent in their own sight.--Isa. v, 21.

24

THE FOURTH COMMANDMENT

1. Remember the Sabbath Day to keep it holy.
2. Six days shalt thou labor and do all thy work. But the seventh day is the Sabbath of the Lord thy God. On it, thou shalt not do any work, neither thou, nor thy son, nor thy daughter, nor thy man-servant, nor thy maid-servant, nor thy cattle, nor thy stranger that is within thy gates. For in six days the Lord made the heavens and the earth, the sea, and all that is in them, and rested on the seventh day; wherefore the Lord blessed the Sabbath day and hallowed it.
3. The Sabbath is for rest from work of all kinds and for a day for special religious duties.
4. These religious duties include family worship, or attendance at a House of Prayer; sacred readings, which mean reading the Bible or any religious book, or hearing a sermon.
5. The Sabbath is the first of the six assembly days or seasons commanded by the Lord (see Chapter xii, No. 9) for holy assembly and readings.
6. The remainder of the Sabbath day after these sacred duties may be devoted to any recreation that is in keeping with the sanctity of the day, which does not involve work for us or our employes, and which does not fatigue the body or the mind.
*7. The institution of the Sabbath closes the Bible account of the creation of the world. This shows, first, that the Sabbath is part of God's plan of creation; secondly, that the seventh-day Sabbath is binding upon all mankind and not upon Jews only.
8. We have three natures, physical, mental and spiritual. Our physical and mental natures are constantly employed during the six days of work. The seventh day, or Sabbath, gives them rest and opportunity to be refreshed. Our

spiritual nature is to be specially attended to on the seventh day, when our ordinary work will not interrupt or prevent.

9. Physical and mental powers alone cannot build character or ensure happiness. Spiritual development is also needed. Hence the Sabbath is necessary for our happiness. And as God created earth to be a scene of human happiness as well as righteousness, the institution of the Sabbath was a necessary part of His plan of creation.

10. To pass the Sabbath Day as merely a day of leisure or for rest from work is to misunderstand the true sacredness of the day. The Sabbath is not properly observed unless we utilise some portion of it to bring our souls nearer to God by communion with Him; that is, by worship, or by sacred exercises, etc.

11. The keeping of the Sabbath is connected with the commands to reverence the sanctuary and to respect our parents, implying that the Sabbath is a day when respect should be shown to the sanctuary or place of worship by our attending service, and to our parents by gathering around them in the home.

12. The weekly gathering in the place of worship helps to unite us as a congregation or community. The weekly gathering in the home helps to unite us as a family.

BIBLE QUOTATIONS.

3. Six days shalt thou do thy work and on the seventh day thou shalt rest; that thine ox and thine ass may rest, and the son of thy handmaid and the stranger may be refreshed.—Exod. xxiii, 12.

The seventh day is the Sabbath of the Lord thy God; on it thou shalt not do any work, thou, nor thy son, nor thy maid-servant, nor thine ox, nor thine ass, nor any of thy cattle, nor thy stranger that is within thy gates; that thy manservant and thy maidservant may rest as well as thou.—Deut. v, 14.

And it shall come to pass that . . . . from one Sabbath to another, shall all flesh come to worship before Me, saith the Lord.—Isa. lxvi, 23.

5. See Chapter xii, Holy Days and Festivals, quotation 3.

6. If thou turn away thy foot from the Sabbath, from doing thy pleasure on My holy day; and, call the Sabbath a delight, the holy of the Lord, honorable; and shall honor Him, not doing thine own ways, nor finding thine own pleasure, nor speaking vain words, then shalt thou delight thyself in the Lord.—Isa. lviii, 13, 14.

7. And the heavens and the earth were finished, and all their host . . . . And God blessed the seventh day and sanctified it; because that on it He ceased from all His work which God created to make.—Gen. ii, 1-3.

9. Not by bread alone, but by all that proceedeth out of the mouth of the Lord, doth man live.—Deut. viii, 3.

11. Ye shall keep My Sabbaths and reverence My Sanctuary. I am the Lord. —Levit. xxvi, 2.

Ye shall respect every one his father and his mother and keep My Sabbaths. I am the Lord your God.—Levit. xix, 3.

25

THE FIFTH COMMANDMENT

Honor thy father and thy mother that thy days may be lengthened, in the land which the Lord thy God giveth thee.

1. Our parents love us, they sacrifice themselves, and think and work only for our benefit. We must therefore love them in return and honor them.
2. We honor them by always respecting them and by always cheerfully obeying their wishes.
3. We must honor their memory when they are dead. For us to do what they would disapprove of were they living, is to insult their memory.
4. Just as we are to honor our parents for what they are to us and what they do for us, so we must honor all who by reason of age, duties or position, deserve our respect.
5. We must honor ministers of religion who teach us our holiest duties by their instruction and example.
6. We must honor the aged, and "rise up before the hoary head."
7. We must honor the learned because of their experience or knowledge.
8. We must respect our teachers and those who are in authority by reason of their position.
*9. To honor parents, ministers of religion, the aged, the learned, our teachers and authorities is a sign of the highest type of true manliness and of true womanliness.
10. Respect for parents is essential to the welfare of society. As the state is founded upon society, respect to parents becomes of the highest importance. Hence the expression "that thy days may be lengthened in the land"—for no

nation can be long in its land if respect is not shown to parents and to all to whom honor is due.

11. Anarchy, or the absence of respect for authority, always brings ruin.

12. Respect for all the authorities is insisted upon in the Bible. Rulers, judges—all officials must be treated with due deference. It is even forbidden to speak disparagingly of them.

BIBLE QUOTATIONS.

1. Honor thy father and thy mother, as the Lord thy God hath commanded thee; that thy days may be prolonged, and that it may go well with thee, in the land which the Lord thy God giveth thee.—Deut. v, 16.

5. Let there be peace to those who love thy law.—Psalm cxix, 165.

6. Thou shalt rise up before the hoary head and thou shalt honor the face of the old.—Lev. xix, 30.

7. Bow down thine ear and hear the words of the wise.—Prov. xxii, 17.

8. From all my teachers I gain understanding.—Psalms cxix, 99.

My son, fear thou the Lord and the king. Meddle not with them that love change.—Prov. xxiv, 21.

12. Curse not the ruler, no, not in thy thought.—Eccles. x, 20.

Thou shalt not curse the authorities.—Ex. xxii, 28.

Thou shalt not curse a ruler among thy people.—Ex. xxii, 28.

26

THE SIXTH COMMANDMENT

Thou shalt not murder.

1. Human life is sacred. We may not take a man's life unless he is a murderer or guilty of some other capital offence.
2. Wars are not countenanced by our religion, except to defend our liberties, lives or homes or to stamp out certain crimes.
3. We may not kill a man's good name or reputation, nor attack his honor.
4. We do so when we act as tale-bearer or slanderer.
*5. We may not kill a man's business.
6. We do this by speaking ill of him, by taking advantage of him, by taking his trade away from him, or by taking from him the last fraction of what he owes us, if by so doing we ruin him.
7. Ignorance on our part is no excuse. We must make it our business to know what we ought to know.
8. Jewish law makes it very difficult to inflict the penalty of death by decision of a court.
9. If, after all the precautions, the sentence of death be pronounced, the culprit is drugged before the penalty is inflicted, so as not to be conscious of the pain of execution.
10. Respect for human life carries with it respect for any one's livelihood. We may not make it hard for others to live by reason of our own greed.

BIBLE QUOTATIONS.

2. But God said unto me, Thou shalt not build a house for My name, because thou hast been a man of war and hast shed blood.—I. Ch. xxviii, 3.

3. Devise not evil against thy neighbor.—Prov. iii, 29.

4. Whoso secretly slandereth his neighbor, him will I cut off.—Psalm ci, 5.

6. I will not turn away the punishment of them . . . that pant after the dust of the earth on the head of the poor.—Amos ii, 5-7.

My lips shall not speak wickedness, nor my tongue utter deceit.—Psalm xxvii, 4.

Thou shalt not stand up against the blood of thy neighbor.—Levit. xix, 16.

The innocent and the righteous slay thou not; for I will not justify the wicked.—Lev. xxiii, 7.

The Lord hateth hands that shed innocent blood.—Prov. vi, 16-17.

7. If thou forbear to rescue those that are doomed to death and nigh to be slain; if thou sayest, Lo, we knew it not, doth not He who weigheth the heart consider it? And He that keepeth thy soul, doth not He know it? And shall He not render to every man according to his works?—Prov. xxiv, 11-12.

10. Woe unto them that join house to house, that lay field to field, till there be no place, that there may be placed alone in the midst of the earth.—Isa. v, 8.

He that withholdeth corn, the people shall curse him.—Prov. xi, 26.

27

THE SEVENTH COMMANDMENT

Thou shalt not commit adultery.

1. This forbids a man marrying another man's wife or a woman marrying another woman's husband.
2. Because husband and wife must give their complete love to each other and must seek each other's happiness unceasingly. And they must give their undivided and constant care to their children.
3. This commandment includes all the commands to lead pure lives.
4. Our thoughts must be pure; then our words and deeds will be pure.
*5. Indecent conduct destroys true manliness or true womanliness of character.
6. No honorable or God-fearing man ever uses indecent words.
7. Modesty is the priceless ornament of true manhood and womanhood.
8. We are forbidden to marry certain near relatives.
9. Because our children would be weak mentally or physically or both; or they would be born deformed.
10. Their lives and the lives of those around them would then be saddened, and their happiness would always be incomplete.
11. Holiness of life is the aim of our religion.
12. Therefore the high-priest, when officiating on the most sacred occasions, wore on his forehead, opposite the brain, the seat of thought, a plate on which was inscribed the sentence "Holy to the Lord." (See *Chap. viii.*)
13. Our conduct must be "Holy to the Lord."

BIBLE QUOTATIONS.

3. Ye shall be holy, for I, the Lord your God, am holy.—Lev. xix, 1.

4. Who shall ascend to the mountain of the Lord, and who shall stand in His holy place? He that hath innocent hands and a pure heart.—Psalm xxiv, 3-4.

Create in me a pure heart, and renew a right spirit within me.—Psalm li, 10.

The thoughts of the wicked are an abomination unto the Lord.—Prov. xv, 26.

The thought of folly is sin.—Prov. xxiv, 9.

I, the Lord, search the heart.—Jer. xvii, 10.

Search me, O God, and know my heart; try me and know my innermost thoughts, and see if there be any wicked way in me, and lead me in the way of eternity.—Psalm cxxxix, 23-24.

5. Turn ye now every one from his evil way, and make your ways and your doings good.—Jerem. xviii, 11.

6. The lips of the righteous know what is acceptable; but the mouth of the wicked speaketh frowardness.—Prov. x, 32.

7. He hath shown thee, O man, what is good. And what doth the Lord require of thee, but to do justly, and to love mercy, and to walk modestly with thy God.—Micah vi, 8.

As a jewel of gold in a swine's nose, so is a fair woman without discretion.—Prov. xi, 22.

28

THE EIGHTH COMMANDMENT

Thou shalt not steal.

1. This forbids us taking anything wrongfully.
2. We are commanded to be scrupulously honest and honorable in all our dealings.
3. We may not cheat, nor deceive, nor deal falsely, nor lie one to another.
4. We may not steal anyone's honor or good name by slander.
5. We may not steal anyone's confidence; that is, gain a person's trust and then betray it.
6. We rob God when we withhold from Him our "tithes and offerings"
7. Tithe means the tenth part. The tenth part of our income should be devoted to charity or to other service of God.
8. An offering in Hebrew is called "Korban." The word means "a drawing near," "an approach." Any righteous act by which we draw near to God, any sacrifice of self for holy purpose, is an offering or sacrifice in the Bible sense of the word.
9. It is not what we give, nor the value of what we give, it is not what a sacrifice costs us that God regards. It is the motive that impels us which alone is acceptable to God and which alone can bring our souls near to Him.
10. God knows what we can afford to give and what sacrifice of time, strength or thought we can make for His sake or for our fellow-being.
11. To excuse ourselves from giving or from helping to the fullest extent of our powers, is trying to deceive God. He knows our hearts.
*12. We may not rob ourselves. We rob ourselves of health when we disobey the laws of food, exercise or proper rest. Long life, well lived, is a blessing.

13. We rob ourselves of the respect due to us when we are guilty of wrong-doing.

14. We rob ourselves of true happiness when, by reason of our disobedience, we are not at peace with God.

15. We rob the poor when we do not give in charity what God knows we can afford to give.

16. Stealing a human being and selling him into slavery is a capital crime in our religion.

17. An escaped slave may not be given back to his former owner.

BIBLE QUOTATIONS.

2. Keep thee far from a false matter.—Exod. xxii, 7.

Lord, who shall abide in Thy tabernacle? Who shall dwell in Thy holy hill? He that walketh uprightly, and worketh righteousness, and speaketh the truth in his heart.—Psalm xv, 1-2.

He that backbiteth not with his tongue, nor doeth evil to his neighbor, nor taketh up a reproach against his neighbor. 3.

Who shall ascend into the hill of the Lord? or who shall stand in His holy place? He that hath clean hands and a pure heart; who hath not lifted up his soul unto vanity, nor sworn deceitfully.—Psalm xxiv, 3-4.

3. Ye shall not steal, neither deal falsely, neither lie one to another.—Levit. xix, 11.

Thou shalt not defraud thy neighbor, neither rob him.—Levit. xix, 13.

Thou shalt have a perfect, and a just weight; a perfect and a just measure shalt thou have.—Deut. xxv, 15.

4. He that uttereth a slander is a fool.—Prov. x, 18.

Death and life are in the power of the tongue.—Prov. xviii, 21.

5. And Absalom stole the hearts of the men of Israel.—II. Sam. xv, 6.

6. Will a man rob God? Yet ye have robbed Me. But ye say, Wherein have we robbed Thee? In tithes and offerings.—Mal. iii, 8.

7. The tenth part shall be holy to the Lord.—Levit. xxvii, 32.

8. Behold to obey is better than sacrifice, and to hearken than the fat of rams.—I. Sam. xv, 22.

Deal out thy bread to the hungry, bring the outcast poor to thy house, clothe them that need to be clothed, hide not thyself from thine own flesh.—Isa. lviii, 7.

I am the Lord who exerciseth loving-kindness, judgment and righteousness on earth, for in these things I delight, saith the Lord.—Jerem. ix, 24.

9. He who formeth their heart alike, understandeth all their works.—Psalm xxxiii, 15.

The Lord looketh on the heart.—I. Sam. xvi, 7.

I know also, O my God, that Thou triest the heart.—I. Chron. xxix, 17.

10. I will not offer offerings unto the Lord my God of that which doth cost me nothing.—II. Sam. xxiv, 24.

All things come of Thee, and of Thine own do we give Thee.—I. Chron. xxix, 14.

What shall I render unto the Lord for all His benefits towards me.—Psalm cxvi, 12.

When ye offer a sacrifice of thanksgiving unto the Lord, offer it willingly.—Levit. xxii, 29.

(These punishments will overtake thee) . . . . because thou servedst not the Lord thy God with joyfulness and with gladness of heart, for the abundance of all things.—Deut. xxvii, 47.

11. I, the Lord, search the heart.—Jerem. xvii, 10.

12. Teach us to number our days.—Psalm xc, 12.

This shall ye eat . . . . This shall ye not eat . . . . Do not defile yourselves.—Levit. x, 2, 9, 13, 42, 44, etc.

O my God, take me not away in the midst of my days.—Psalm cii, 24.

With long life will I satisfy him.—Psalm xci, 15.

O Lord, by these things men live, and in all these things is the life of my spirit.—Isa. xxxviii, 16.

13. The wrongdoer cometh to shame.—Prov. xiii, 5.

14. There is no peace, saith my God, to the wicked.—Isa. lvii, 21.

15. If there be among you a poor man . . . . thou shalt not harden thine heart, nor shut thy hand from thy poor brother.—Deut. xv, 7.

But thou shalt open thy hand wide unto him; thou shalt surely lend him sufficient for his need in that which he lacketh.—Deut. xv, 8.

Thou shalt surely give him, and thine heart shall not be grieved when thou givest unto him. Because for this the Lord thy God will bless thee in all thy works, and in all which thou puttest thine hand unto.—Deut. xv, 10.

Blessed is the man that considereth the poor.—Psalm xli, 1.

He that hath mercy on the poor, happy is he.—Prov. xiv, 21.

He that hath pity on the poor lendeth unto the Lord, and that which he hath given him will He pay him again.—Prov. xix, 17.

He that giveth to the poor shall not lack, but he that hideth his eyes shall have many a sorrow.—Prov. xxviii, 27.

He that oppresseth the poor reproacheth his Maker, but he that honoreth Him is kind to the poor.—Prov. xv, 31.

Whoso mocketh the poor reproacheth his Maker, and he that is glad at calumnies shall not be unpunished.—Prov. xvii, 5.

16. He that stealeth a man and selleth him, and he be found in his hand, he shall surely die.—Exod. xxi, 16.

17. Thou shalt not deliver unto his master the servant who hath escaped from his master unto thee.—Deut. xxiii, 15.

He shall dwell with thee, even among thee, in the place which he shall choose, in one of thy gates where it liketh him best; thou shalt not oppress him. —Deut. xxiii, 16.

29

THE NINTH COMMANDMENT

**Thou shalt not bear false
witness against thy neighbor.**

1. This commandment commands us to speak the truth about each other at all times.
2. It forbids us to deceive our neighbor, for deception means expressing what is false.
3. It forbids us to make untruthful excuses, excuses which are only partly true, or to exaggerate or to conceal any part of the truth.
4. It commands us to keep our word. Whatever we promise to do, we must do. Otherwise we deceive people by our words, and at the same time bear witness against ourselves; for we prove ourselves untruthful.
5. We also bear false witness against ourselves when we pretend to be what we are not.
*6. We bear false witness against our neighbor when we are guilty of hypocrisy, backbiting, slur, unjust criticism, unkind or inconsiderate remarks that are undeserved, or silently hear such without protest.
7. We sometimes destroy a person's reputation or steal from him respect due to him or bear false witness against him, by a mere sign or gesture, by a shrug or a mockery, and even by keeping silence when his character is assailed.
8. We also bear false witness against our neighbor when, while pretending to joke, we say or intimate something against his character or ability.
9. Those who pull others to pieces in our presence will pull us to pieces in our absence.
10. Never trust a backbiter.

11. We bear false witness against ourselves, our neighbor and our God when we refuse help which we can afford to give.

12. Also if we refuse to subscribe to charities or to communal institutions when we do not hesitate to spend money for our own pleasure.

13. And when without sufficient excuse, we stay away from public worship on the days on which God commands us to assemble—Sabbaths, Rosh Hashana or New Year, Kipur or Day of Atonement, Pesach or Passover, Shabuoth or Feast of Weeks and Succoth or Tabernacles.

14. We bear false witness against our religion when we call ourselves Jews of Jewesses while we live unjewish lives or break Jewish Law.

15. We bear false witness against our God when we do not stand up for God and the Right.

BIBLE QUOTATIONS.

1. Speak ye, everyone, the truth to his neighbor. Execute the judgment of truth and peace in your gates.—Zech. viii, 16.

Love ye the truth and the peace.—Zech. viii, 19.

2. The vile person speaketh what is vile, his heart contrives iniquity, to practise hypocrisy.—Isa. xxxii, 6.

I hate every false way.—Psalm cxix, 104.

The Lord hateth a false witness that speaketh lies, and him that soweth discord among brethren.—Prov. vi, 6, 19.

3. Let them hear and say, it is the truth.—Isa. xliii, 9.

Say nothing but the truth.—II. Kings xviii, 15.

Buy the truth and sell it not.—Prov. xxiii, 23.

4. That which goeth out of thy lips thou shalt keep and do.—Deut. xxiii, 23.

5. My words shall not be false.—Job xxxvi, 4.

6. What is the hope of the hypocrite, though he hath gained, when God taketh away his soul?—Job xxvii, 8.

Will God hear his cry when trouble cometh upon him?—Job xxvii, 9.

The north wind driveth away rain; so an angry countenance a backbiting tongue.—Prov. xxv, 23.

A wounded spirit who can bear?—Prov. xviii, 14.

7. They laughed them to scorn and mocked them; nevertheless some of Asher, Menasseh and Zebulon humbled themselves.—II. Chron. xxx, 11.

They mocked the messengers of God and despised his words and misused His prophets.—II. Chron. xxxvi, 16.

8. As a madman who casteth firebrands, arrows and death, so is he that deceiveth his neighbor and saith, am I not in sport?—Prov. xxvi, 18, 19.

10. Trust not in lying words.—Jerem. vii, 4.

11. Withhold not good from them to whom it is due, when it is in the power of thine hand to do it.—Prov. iii, 27.

12. Speak unto the children of Israel, that they bring Me an offering, of

everyone that giveth it willingly with his heart ye shall take My offering.—Exod. xxv, 2.

13. These are the assembly days of the Lord, even holy convocations, ye shall proclaim in their seasons.—Lev. xxiii, 4.

14. Ye say, the table of the Lord is contemptible.—Mal. i, 7.

But ye profane My name, in that ye say, the table of the Lord is polluted, and the fruit thereof, even His meat, is contemptible.—Mal. i, 12.

Ye say also, what a weariness it is.—Mal. i, 13.

Ye say, It is vain to serve God, and what profit is it that we keep His ordinances, and that we walk mournfully before the Lord of Hosts?—Mal. iii, 14.

30

THE TENTH COMMANDMENT

Thou shalt not covet thy neighbor's house, thou shalt not covet thy neighbor's wife, nor his manservant, nor his maidservant, nor his ox, nor his ass, nor anything that is thy neighbor's.

1. To desire anything that our neighbor has, makes us discontented and leads us to envy or jealousy.
2. It may also lead us into committing a crime in order to gain what we covet.
3. We must be contented with what God has given us.
4. Happiness does not depend upon what we have, but upon what we are.
5. We cannot be happy if we are envious or jealous.
*6. Wealth brings temptations and usually leads to selfishness. The children of wealthy parents are especially liable to grow up selfish, through indulgence or through ignorance of others' wants. The better qualities of their manhood or womanhood are sometimes undeveloped.
7. This command also teaches that we can sin in thought, since we can sin by coveting or wishing for anything not ours.
8. Unjust thoughts, impure thoughts, and all other sinful thoughts must be instantly, constantly and rigorously suppressed.
9. Otherwise they will grow stronger and stronger.
10. Evil thoughts if unchecked, will surely become evil deeds.
11. We are what our thoughts are. Pure and noble thoughts mean pure and noble character. Unrighteous thoughts will mean unrighteous lives.
12. We cannot help wrong thoughts coming to us. But we can help allowing them to remain in our minds.

13. We can conquer evil thoughts. God told Cain that we can subdue sin instead of sin conquering us.

14. "Take great care of your souls," is a Bible command. We cannot keep our souls pure if we indulge in evil thoughts.

BIBLE QUOTATIONS.

1. Woe unto him that coveteth.—Hab. ii, 9.

Give me neither property nor riches, feed me with the food assigned to me.—Prov. xxx, 9.

Envy slayeth the silly person.—Job v, 2.

Fury is cruel and anger is outrageous, but who is able to stand before envy? Jealousy is cruel as the grave.—Song of Solomon viii, 6.

HOW COVETING LED TO CRIME.

2. Now Naboth of Jezreel had a vineyard.

And Ahab spake unto Naboth saying, Give me thy vineyard, that I may have it for a garden of herbs . . . . And Naboth said to Ahab, the Lord forbid it me, that I should give the inheritance of my fathers unto thee. And Ahab went to his house, heavy and displeased . . . . But Jezebel, his wife, came to him and said, "Why is thy spirit so sad, that thou eatest no bread?" And he told her. And she said, "Dost thou govern the kingdom? Arise, eat, be merry, I will give thee Naboth's vineyard." So she wrote letters in Ahab's name, and sealed with his seal, to the elders and nobles in Naboth's city, saying, "Proclaim a fast, set Naboth on high, and set two men, *men* of no character, to witness against him saying, Thou didst blaspheme God and the king. Then carry him out and stone him, that he die . . . ." And they did so, and sent to Jezebel, saying, Naboth is stoned and is dead. And she said to Ahab, Arise and take Naboth's vineyard, for he is dead. And Ahab rose up to go to Naboth's vineyard and to possess it.

And the word of the Lord came to Elijah the Tishbite. Arise, go, meet Ahab. Behold, he is in Naboth's vineyard, whither he has gone to possess it. And thou shalt speak unto him saying, Thus saith the Lord, Hast thou killed and also taken possession . . . . In the place where the dogs licked the blood of Naboth shall dogs lick thy blood, even thine . . . . And of Jezebel He spake saying, the dogs shall eat Jezebel by the walls of Jezreel.—I. Kings xxi.

3. Better is a little with the fear of the Lord, than great treasure and trouble therewith.—Prov. xv, 16.

Better is a dinner of herbs where love is, than a stalled ox and hatred therewith.—Prov. xv, 17.

4. I know of a surety that it shall be well with them who are God-fearing, who fear before Him.—Eccles. viii, 12.

5. They shall be ashamed for their envy.—Isa. xxvi, 11.

Jealousy is the rage of man.—Prov. vi, 34.

6. Let not the rich man glory in his riches, . . . but let him that glorieth glory

in this, that he understandeth and knoweth Me, that I am the Lord who exerciseth loving-kindness, judgment and righteousness on earth; for in these things, I delight, saith the Lord.—Jerem. ix, 23, 24.

The rich man is wise in his own conceit.—Prov. xxviii, 11.
The Lord looketh on the heart.—I Sam. xvi, 7.
Let the man of iniquity forsake his thoughts.—Isa. lv, 7.
Thou, O Lord, knowest me.—Jerem. xii, 2.
I, the Lord, search the heart.—Jerem. xvii, 10.
Woe unto them that devise iniquity.—Micah ii, 1.
Thou understandeth my thought afar off.—Psalm cxxxix, 2.
O God, create in me a clean heart, and renew a right spirit within me.—Psalm li, 10.

Thoughts of evil are an abomination unto the Lord.—Prov. xv, 26.

8. Take heed that there be not a base thought in thy heart.—Deut. xv, 9.

HOW EVIL THOUGHTS LED TO MURDER.

10. And David saw a woman very beautiful to look upon. And he sent and enquired about her. And one said, is she not Bathsheba, the wife of Uriah, the Hittite. But David sent messengers and took her. And David wrote a letter to Joab and sent it by the hand of Uriah, saying, Set ye Uriah in the forefront of the hottest battle and retire ye from him, that he may be smitten and die. And Joab assigned him to a place where he knew were mighty men. And the men of the city went out and fought with Joab, and there fell of the people of David, and Uriah the Hittite died. And Joab sent and told David all concerning the war, and charged the messenger to say, "thy servant, Uriah the Hittite is dead also." And the messenger told David all that Joab sent him for. And David said, This shalt thou say unto Joab, Let not this thing displease thee, for the sword devoureth one as well as another . . . . And Bathsheba mourned her husband . . . . And David sent and fetched her and she became his wife. But the thing that David had done displeased the Lord. And the Lord sent Nathan unto David, and he said unto him, There were two men in one city, the one rich and the other poor. The rich man had exceeding many flocks and herds. But the poor man had nothing, save one little ewe-lamb, which he had bought and nourished up; and it grew up together with him, and with his children; it did eat of his own meat and drank of his own cup, and lay in his bosom, and was unto him as a daughter. And there came a traveler unto the rich man, and he spared to take of his own flock and of his own herd, to dress for the wayfaring man that was come unto him; but took the poor man's lamb, and dressed it for the man that was come to him.

And David's anger was greatly kindled against the man, and he said to Nathan, As the Lord liveth, the man that hath done this shall surely die.

And he shall restore the lamb fourfold, because he did this thing and because he had no pity.

And Nathan said to David, Thou art the man!

Thus saith the Lord God of Israel, I anointed thee king, I delivered thee from Saul, I gave thee thy master's house and wives, the house of Israel and Judah, and if that were too little, I would have given thee more.

Wherefore hast thou despised the commandment of the Lord, to do evil in his sight? Thou hast killed Uriah the Hittite, and hast taken his wife to be thy wife.

Therefore the sword shall never leave thine house. Behold, I will raise up evil against thee out of thine own house.

And David said unto Nathan, I have sinned against the Lord.—II. Sam. xii, 13.

11. As he thinketh in his heart, so is he.—Prov. xxiii, 7.

13. If thou doest not well, sin croucheth at the door. And unto thee is its desire, but thou shouldst rule over it.—Gen. iv, 7.

14. Take heed to thyself, and keep thy soul diligently.—Deut. iv, 9.

PART II

THE CREED.

31

THE MEANING OF THE CREEDS

1. Our creeds tell us what we believe as Hebrews.
2. They are all taken from the Bible teachings as explained by our sages.
3. When we speak of the Jewish creeds we usually mean those drawn up by a great sage, named Maimonides, who was born in Spain in the year 1135.
4. They are as follows:

1. God is the Creator and Governor of the universe and all that is therein.
2. He is a unity.
3. He has no bodily form.
4. He is eternal.
5. He is the only Being whom we may worship.
6. All the words of the prophets are true.
7. Moses is the chief of the prophets.
8. The Law which we now have is the same that was given to Moses.
9. It never has been changed for another Law and never will be changed.
10. God knows all our thoughts and actions.
11. Those who obey His commandments will receive reward. Those who disobey will reap the penalty.
12. The Messiah will come and establish peace and happiness on earth.
13. After death we live again in another life.

32

THE FIRST CREED.

I believe with a perfect faith that the Creator, blessed be His name, is the Creator and Governor of all Creation, and that He alone has made, does make and ever will make, all things.

1. God is the Creator and Governor of the universe and all that is therein.
2. The universe and all that is therein, we call Nature.
3. The more we study Nature and learn the wonders of Creation the more we marvel at the magnificence, the power and the goodness of God, the Creator of all.
4. His magnificence and power make us reverent. His goodness makes us grateful.
5. This knowledge of God's magnificence, power and goodness, little as it is that we can know, leads us through our reverence for Him and our gratitude to Him, to love Him and to serve Him.
6. To the Creator of all good, to Him who provides for mankind's wants, to the Governor or guide of all, we can never be sufficiently grateful. To His love and guidance we can always safely commit our dear ones and ourselves, knowing that He will help us if we are deserving.
7. The order and beauty of Nature also prove the existence of a master mind or intelligence. The order of the planets and their motions; the order of the seasons and tides; the laws which we call the laws of Nature; all *these* prove the existence of a supreme intelligence. That Supreme Intelligence is God.
8. Not less does the beauty of Nature appeal to us. Nature is very beautiful, whether we view it in the different colors of the stars, the beautiful motion of the ocean, the wonderful grace of animals, birds and fishes, the colors of foliage and flowers—all these are beautiful. They are the works of a

Creator who knows that a consciousness of beauty is an essential of human happiness. God created the world, and He intended it to be a world of happiness.

9. God is the Author of all life.

10. What we call life, is a something separate from the matter it animates. *That something* comes from God just as He is the Creator of the material parts also. Furthermore, the matter or substance of which anything is composed, shows the design of a supreme intelligence. For every particle is fitted for its duty.

11. Every particle, after its function has ceased, becomes of use in some other way. Nothing is wasted. What we call waste, is only matter out of place. There is a God who is the Creator of everything and of every atom of everything, who fits it to perform its function and who watches over and governs its changes from one form into another.

12. The knowledge of the nature of God should help us to try to deserve the blessing and protection of such a good and loving Being. It will also lead us to trust in His power to help us, since He is all-powerful, almighty or omnipotent.

13. And as Creator and Renewer of the Universe He is omnipresent, or present everywhere. Therefore, wherever we are, we can speak to Him in prayer.

14. To know God, to recognize Him as Creator, is useless, unless our knowledge of Him influences our conduct.

BIBLE QUOTATIONS.

1. Thus saith God the Lord, He that created the heavens and stretched them out: He that spread forth the earth and that which cometh out of it; He that giveth breath unto the people upon it, and spirit to them that walk therein.—Isa. xlii, 5.

3. Job xxvi speaks of some of the wonders of the Creator, the forms of creatures under the vast waters (v. 5); the supervision of the Creator in every abyss (v. 6); the mysteries of ether or space, the mystery of gravitation (v. 7); the laws of rain (v. 8); the laws of the clouds that shroud heaven, His throne (v. 9); the laws of the tides and the waters (v. 10); the crash of thunder and the laws of the tempest (v. 11); the storm on the ocean and the hurling back of its proud billows (v. 12); the heavens adorned with the countless orbs (v. 13); the serpent-like streak across them (v. 13)—"Lo!" exclaims Job, "these are but whispers of His ways; but how little a portion thus is heard of Him? But the thunder of His power who can understand?" (v. 14).

Chapter xxxviii, etc., is also a magnificent exposition of God's tremendous power.

4. Shout joyfully unto God, all ye lands; Sing forth the glory of His name; make His praise glorious. Say unto God, How awe-inspiring are Thy Works!—Psalm lxvi, 1-3.

Be thankful unto Him and bless His name, for the Lord is good, His mercy is eternal.—Psalm c, 4.

5. I love the Lord because He hath heard my supplications.... What shall I render unto the Lord for all His benefits towards me? I will offer unto Thee the sacrifice of thanksgiving, and will call upon the Name of the Lord.—Psalm, cxvi, 1, 5, 12, 17.

6. The Lord will preserve thee from all evil; He will preserve thy soul.—Psalm cxxi, 7.

God be gracious unto thee, my son.—Gen. xliii, 29.

7. He made the earth by His power; He established the universe by His wisdom, and He stretched out the heavens by His discretion.—Jer. li, 15.

He hath made everything beautiful.—Eccles. iii, 11.

Happy is the people that is thus; Happy is the people whose God is the Lord.—Psalm cxliv, 15.

9. See ye now that I, even I, am He, and there is no God with Me; I kill and I make alive.—Deut. xxxii, 39.

In His hand is the soul of every living thing and the breath of all mankind.—Job xii, 10.

11. Thou takest away their breath; they die and return to their dust. Thou sendest forth Thy spirit; they are created; and Thou renewest the face of earth.—Psalm civ, 29, 30.

Fear thou not, for I am with thee; be not dismayed, for I am thy God; I will strengthen thee; yea, I will help thee; yea, I will uphold thee with the right hand of My righteousness.—Isa. xli, 10.

13. Whither shall I go from Thy spirit, or whither shall I flee from Thy presence?

If I ascend up into heaven, Thou art there; if I make my bed in the grave, Thou art there.

If I take the wings of the morning, and dwell in the uttermost parts of the sea;

Even there shall Thy right hand lead me, and Thy right hand shall hold me.

If I say, surely the darkness shall cover me; even the night shall be light about me,

Yea, the darkness hideth not from Thee; but the night shineth as the day, the darkness and the light are both alike to Thee.—Psalm cxxxix, 7-12.

14. Unto the wicked God saith, what hast thou to do to declare My statutes, or that thou shouldst take My covenant in thy mouth?—Psalm 1, 16.

Wherefore the Lord said, Forasmuch as this people draw near Me with their mouth, and with their lips do honour Me, but have removed their heart far from Me, and their reverence of Me is taught by precepts of men. Therefore, behold I will proceed to do a marvellous work among this people, even a marvellous work and a wonder.—Isa. xxix, 13, 14.

33

THE SECOND CREED.

**I believe with a perfect faith that the Creator,
Blessed be His name, is a unity, and that there is no unity like His whatever.
And that He alone is our God who was, who is, and who will ever be**

1. The meaning of this creed is that God is one, no being is joined with Him, and there is no God except Him.

2. Though one may pray to God on behalf of another, we really need no intercessor. We can go direct to God ourselves with our prayers to ask for Help, Guidance, Pardon or whatever we happen to need.

3. No other being can save us from sin or from its evil consequences. God is the only Savior. Nor can the prayers even of those who love us save us or help us if we are undeserving of God's grace.

4. To associate any being with Him, to imagine that any other being has God-like powers, or to pray to any other being, is an insult to Him. It is idolatry. It is disloyalty to God.

5. He who, knowing God, prays to any other being or allows himself to be blessed in the name of any other being, is a traitor to God.

6. We Hebrews have always been monotheists, or believers in one God, even though many of our ancestors turned to idolatry, for which the true Hebrews and the prophets, invariably condemned them.

We have also always been monolatrists or worshippers of one God, even though many of our ancestors believed in the existence of other gods, and even worshipped them; for which the true Hebrews and the prophets, invariably condemned them.

7. The true Hebrews, from Abraham to our own day, have always believed in the one only God and have always worshipped the one only God.

BIBLE QUOTATIONS.

1. Hear, O Israel, the Lord our God, the Lord is One.—Deut. vi, 4.

There is none like Me on all the earth.—Exod. ix, 14.

Look unto Me and be saved, all ends of the earth, for I am God, and there is none else.—Is. xlv, 22.

Before me there was no God formed, neither shall there be after Me.—Isa. xliii, 10.

I am the Lord, that is My name, and My glory I will not give to another.—Is. xlii, 8.

There is no God *besides Me*. I know not any.—Is. xliv, 8.

Thou art God alone.—Psalm lxxxvi, 10.

He is God, there is none else.—I. Kings, viii, 60.

That all the peoples of the earth may know that the Lord He is God, there is none else.—I. Kings, viii, 50.

I am the Lord, and there is none else, there is no God besides Me.—Is. xlv, 5.

I am God, and there is none else; I am God and there is none like Me.—Is. xlvi, 9.

I, even I am the Lord, and beside Me there is no Saviour.—Is. xliii, 11.

The Lord is the true God.—Jerem. x, 10.

To the end that thou mayest know that I am the Lord in the midst of the earth.—Exod. viii, 22.

Thou shalt know no God but Me, for there is no Saviour besides Me.—Hos. xiii, 4.

2. For He hath not despised nor abhorred the affliction of the afflicted; neither hath He hid His face from him; but when he cried unto Him, He heard.—Psalm xxii, 24.

Let us search and try our ways, and turn again to the Lord.—Lamentations iii, 40.

Return unto Me and I will return unto you.—Mal. iii, 7.

3. He is my Saviour.—II. Sam. xxii, 3.

I am the Lord thy God, the Holy One of Israel, thy Saviour.—Isa. xliii, 3.

O God of Israel, the Saviour.—Isa. xlv, 15.

There is no God else besides Me; a just God and Saviour; there is none beside Me.—Isa. xlv, 21.

Look unto Me and be saved, all the ends of the earth, for I am God, and there is none else.—Isa. xlv, 22.

All flesh shall know that I The Lord am thy Saviour and thy Redeemer, The Mighty One of Jacob.—Isa. xlix, 26.

4. My glory will I not give to another.—Isa. xlii, 8; Isa. xlviii, 11.

He is thy praise.—Deut. x, 21.

O Lord, Thou art my praise.—Jer. xvii, 14.

Thou shalt worship no other God.—Exod. xxxiv, 14.

6. Thou shalt have no other gods before Me.—Exod. xx, 3; Deut. v, 7.

Know therefore this day and reflect in thy heart, that the Lord He is God, in heaven above and on earth beneath there is none else.—Deut. iv, 39.

There is no god with Me.—Deut. xxxii, 39.

I am the first and I am the last, and besides Me there is no God.—Isa. xliv, 6.

7. And he (Abraham) believed in the Lord.—Gen. xv, 6.

And the people reverenced the Lord and they believed in the Lord.—Exod. xiv, 31.

Believe in the Lord your God, so shall ye be established.—II. Chron. xx, 20.

34

THE THIRD CREED.

I believe with a perfect faith that the Creator, blessed be His name, has no bodily form, and bodily conditions cannot affect Him; to nothing whatever can He be compared.

1. God is a Spirit. Therefore He has no bodily form.
2. We may not make any image or anything to represent Him.
3. We know a person by his bodily form and nature. But God, having no bodily form, we can know Him only by His nature.
4. The Bible tells us that we know God when we know that He is the Lord who exerciseth loving-kindness, justice and righteousness on earth, and that He delighteth in these things.
5. We prove that we know Him when we ourselves are thereby inspired to exercise loving-kindness, justice and righteousness, and to delight in these things.
*6. When the Bible says we are created in the image of God, it means not in a bodily but in a spiritual likeness.
7. We are spiritually like Him when we exercise loving-kindness, justice and righteousness and take delight in these things.
8. To be like God we must lead lives that are God-*like or Godly; in other words, we must "walk before God and be perfect."
9. We read in the Bible of God's arm, or hands, or face, etc. These are only expressions to convey ideas in human language for human comprehension. God, being incorporeal, has no corporeal parts.
10. Similarly when we read of His anger, or hatred, or vengeance, etc., we use words expressing human emotions to convey human ideas to human and therefore finite minds.

11. Finite minds cannot comprehend God, the Infinite.

BIBLE QUOTATIONS.

1. For who in Heaven can be compared unto the Lord, who among the mighty can be likened unto the Lord?—Psalm lxxxix, 6.
2. Thou shalt not make unto thyself any graven image or any likeness of anything that is in the heaven above or that is in the earth beneath or that is in the waters under the earth. Thou shalt not bow down thyself to them nor serve them.—Exod. xx, 4, 5.
3. No human being can perceive Me and Live.—Exod. xxxiii, 20.

Touching the Almighty we cannot find Him out. He is excellent in Power and in justice and in abundance of charity. He will not afflict.—Job xxxvii, 23.

4. Let Him that glorieth glory in this, that he understandeth and knoweth Me, that I am the Lord who exerciseth loving kindness, justice and righteousness on earth, for in these things I delight, saith the Lord.—Jerem. ix, 24.
6. And God said let us make man in our image, after our likeness.—Gen. i, 26.
8. Walk before Me and be thou perfect.—Gen. xvii, 1.

Thou shalt be perfect with the Lord thy God.—Deut. xviii, 13.

35

THE FOURTH CREED.

I believe with a perfect faith that the Creator, blessed be His name, is the first and the last.

1. God is eternal.
2. Therefore He will be existing to bring about all His promises for the happiness of Israel and mankind in His own good time.
3. As He is with us in this life, so He will be with us in future life.
*4. The knowledge that God is eternal, especially when coupled with the knowledge that He is omnipotent reconciles us with our trials and sorrows, and solves the puzzles of earthly life and its many seeming difficulties and contradictions.
5. Thus, we observe that the good often suffer misfortune or trial, and the wicked are successful and apparently happy.
6. We know that no one can go through life without tasting sorrows, from the pain of mere disappointment to the agony of bereavement.
7. But God is Eternal, and will, in His own time and in His own way, in this life or in the Future or Eternal Life, show us the meaning and benefits of the sorrows and trials, the difficulties and contradictions.
8. We must have faith in God,
He knows what is best.
He does what is best.
9. The lesson of the book of Job is that earthly life is discipline or training. The discipline is often sorrow, and the training is often trial.
10. But our characters, our lives, should not be made beautiful only by our sorrows and trials. Our joys also should encourage us to consecrate our lives all the more, in order that we may deserve further joys, and our successes

should strengthen and extend our efforts to utilize them more and more for God's glory and mankind's happiness.

11. We human beings proclaim God's glory on earth when our lives demonstrate that our religion is God's influence upon our conduct, and therefore means right words, right deeds and right thoughts.

12. Such religion will also mean that we contribute to human happiness; for God's glory on earth is the happiness of all mankind, His children.

BIBLE QUOTATIONS.

1. The Eternal God is thy refuge.—Deut. xxxiii, 27.

I the Lord, the first and the last, I am He.—Isa. xli, 4.

Before the mountains were brought forth, or ever Thou hadst formed the Earth and the universe, even from everlasting to everlasting, Thou art God.—Psalm xc, 2.

2. I have said and I will do it.

I am the Lord, I will hasten it in its time.—Isa. lx, 22.

3. Though I walk through the valley of the shadow of death, I will not fear evil, for Thou art with me.—Psalm xxiii, 4.

The Lord will guide thee always.—Isa. lviii, 11.

For this God is our God for ever and ever. He will be our guide beyond death.—Psalm xlviii, 14.

4. When thou passeth through the waters, I will be with thee; and through the rivers they shall not overflow thee; when thou walketh through fire, thou shalt not be burned, neither shall flame kindle upon thee. For I am the Lord thy God, the Holy One of Israel thy Saviour.—Isa. xliii, 2, 3.

Fear thou not, for I am with thee: be not dismayed; for I am thy God; I will strengthen thee; yea, I will help thee; yea, I will uphold thee with the right hand of My righteousness.—Isa. xli, 10.

Thou shalt forget thy misery and think of it as waters that have passed away, and thine age shall be clearer than the noonday.—Job xi, 16, 17.

5. O Lord of Hosts, that triest the righteous.—Jerem. xx, 12.

Many are afflictions of the righteous, but the Lord delivereth him from all.—Psalm xxxiv, 19.

Wherefore doth the way of the wicked prosper, wherefore are all they happy that deal very treacherously—Jer. xii, 1.

6. Man is born to trouble, as the sparks fly upward.—Job v, 7.

Man born of woman, is of few days, and full of trouble.—Job xiv, 1.

For all his days are sorrow and his travail grief; yea, his heart taketh not rest in the night. This also is vanity.—Eccles. ii, 23.

What man is he that liveth and doth not see death?—Psalm lxxxix, 48.

Make the mourning, as for an only child, most bitter lamentation.—Jerem. vi, 26.

And Abraham came to mourn for Sarah and to weep for her.—Gen. xxiii, 2.

I sat down and wept, and mourned and fasted and prayed before the God of Heaven.—Nehem. i, 4.

Every one knoweth his own sorrow and his own grief.—2 Chron. vi, 29.

The heart knoweth its own bitterness.—Prov. xiv, 10.

7. The Lord shall give thee rest, from thy sorrow and from thy fear, and from the hard servitude thou wast made to serve.—Isa. xiv, 3.

For Thine eyes are open upon all the ways of the sons of men to give every man according to his ways and according to the fruit of his doings.—Jerem. xxxii, 10.

I know, O Lord, that Thy judgments are right, and that Thou in faithfulness hast afflicted me.—Psalm cxix, 75.

Behold happy is the man whom God correcteth, therefore despise not thou the chastening of the Almighty.—Job v, 17.

Why art thou cast down, O my soul, and why art thou disquieted within me? Hope thou in God for I shall yet praise Him, the Salvation of my face, my God.—Psalm xlii, 5, 11; xliii, 5.

Rest in the Lord and wait patiently for Him.—Psalm xxxvii, 7.

Thou wilt show me the path of life; the fulness of joys in Thy presence; the everlasting happiness at Thy right hand.—Psalm xvi, 11.

And now, O Lord, what wait I for? My hope is in Thee.—Psalm xxxix, 7.

8. The righteous man liveth by his faith.—Hab. ii, 4.

Though he slay me, yet will I trust in Him.—Job xiii, 15.

10. Honor thy Lord with thy substance, and with the first fruits of all thine increase.—Prov. iii, 9.

36

THE FIFTH CREED.

I believe with a perfect faith that to the Creator, blessed be His name, it is proper to pray. And it is not proper to pray to any one else besides Him.

1. We may pray to God only.
2. He is the only God, the only Power, therefore there is no other to whom we can pray.
3. Prayer means speaking to God. It may be Praise, Supplication or Thanksgiving. (See chapter vii.)
4. To speak to God about what is most in our hearts, even as a child speaks to its father, is true prayer.
5. After our regular prayers, it is well to add a short prayer expressing whatever our hearts prompt us to place before God.
6. Prayer must always be said with devotion. This is what the Bible means when it speaks of "lifting up the soul," or "lifting up the heart to God," or "pouring out the soul."
7. God never fails to answer true prayer, unless in His wisdom He thinks it better for us that He should refuse, or if He finds us unworthy through sin.
*8. Prayer is communion with God. It is the expression in worship of what our souls feel.
9. We should offer prayer regularly three times a day, when we rise, when we retire and some time during the day. When we rise we should ask His guidance and help for our coming day's work. When we retire we should thank Him for His protection. During the day we should withdraw from our earthly surroundings for at least a few moments' prayer or communion with Him.
10. But we should also pray at any moment that our heart impels us, in any

emergency or danger, in any moment of sudden trouble or anxiety. We should seek His guidance at all times. God is always ready to hear prayer.

11. We may pray in any proper place, but especially in synagogues or places specially built for worship, and where the associations contribute to devotion.

12. Places of worship should be kept open all day for private prayer by those who wish "to seek the Lord" or to "pour out their hearts before Him."

13. The fixed form of prayers which we say with others, should include or should end with private prayer for our loved ones and ourselves. But in all petitions to God we must pray that His will be done, or that what we ask for may be acceptable to Him, or "Let Him do to me as seemeth good to Him" (II. Sam. xv, 26).

14. This trains us to the habit of prayer. It may be called spiritual exercise or spiritual discipline.

15. Prayer is of little use unless we are conscious of what we say and feel that we are actually speaking to God.

16. After true prayer we feel that we have been near to God.

17. The object of prayer is to bring us near to God.

18. This was the original object of the ancient sacrifices, which were therefore called Korbanoth, or "approachings," from "*Karab*," to come or draw near.

19. We should place before God all our private wants, our sorrows and our perplexities. Nothing that troubles us in our daily lives is so unimportant that we need hesitate to speak to God about it in prayer.

20. Exercising our physical powers gives us increased physical strength. Exercising our mental powers gives us increased mental strength. Exercising our spiritual powers gives us increased spiritual strength. Prayer is an exercise of our spiritual powers. It increases our spiritual strength.

21. Prayer without proper conduct is worse than useless. It is an insult to God.

22. Our prophets condemn prayer, sacrifices, the observance of Sabbath and other Holy Days, and all religious ceremonies, unless our conduct is acceptable to God.

23. Right conduct is everything. Religious forms without right conduct are useless.

24. Unless prayer, Sabbath, Holy Days and all religious ceremonies or forms build up right character, they fail in their purpose.

25. We cannot expect that God will answer our prayers, unless we "do justly, love kindness and walk modestly before Him."

For "He is too pure to look upon iniquity."

26. Prayer in private worship is specially to express private needs or private emotions.

27. Prayer in the synagogue or public place of worship is to express general Jewish needs or emotions which affect all Hebrews. We pray for them and they pray for us. Hence these prayers are in the plural number.

28. Prayer in synagogue also strengthens the bond of union with our

brethren of Israel; and rightly conducted, creates a greater religious sentiment or enthusiasm.

29. Readers and choirs may not pray for us without our hearts responding. They may only pray with us.

30. We must pray for ourselves.

BIBLE QUOTATIONS.

1. Thou shalt worship no other God.—Exod. xxxiv, 14.

Take heed unto yourself lest your heart deceive and ye turn aside and serve other gods and worship them.—Deut. xi, 16.

2. And Hezekiah prayed before the Lord and said, O Lord God of Israel which dwelleth among the Cherubim. Thou art God, even Thou alone.—2 Kings xix, 15.

3. Commit thy way unto the Lord.—Ps. xxxvii, 5.

Cast thy burden upon the Lord. He will sustain thee.—Ps. lv, 22.

What prayer and supplication soever be made by any man, or by any of Thy people Israel, which shall know every man the anguish of his own heart, and spread forth his hands toward this house.

Then hear Thou in heaven Thy dwelling place, and forgive and do, and give to every man according to his ways whose heart Thou knowest; for Thou, even Thou only, knowest the hearts, of all the children of men.—1 Kings viii, 38, 39.

Praise.

O Lord, how manifold are Thy works! In wisdom hast Thou made them all; Earth is full of Thy possessions!—Ps. civ, 24.

Supplication.

Give ear, O Lord, unto my prayer and hearken to the voice of my supplications.—Psalm lxxxvi, 6.

Hear me when I call, O God of my righteousness: Thou didst deliver me when I was in sorrow; O be gracious unto me and hear my prayer.—Ps. iv, 1.

Look down from Thy holy habitation from heaven and bless Thy people Israel.—Deut. xxvi, 15.

Thanksgiving.

When ye offer a thanksgiving offering unto the Lord, offer it willingly.—Levit. xxii, 29.

Offer unto God thanksgiving.—Ps. l, 14.

I will give thanks unto Thee forever.—Ps. xxx, 12.

I will magnify Him with thanksgiving.—Ps. lxix, 30.

I will sacrifice unto Thee with the voice of Thanksgiving.—Jonah ii, 9.

O give thanks unto the Lord for He is good, for His mercy endureth for ever.—Ps. cxxxvi, 1.

4. Thou, O Lord, art our Father, our Redeemer.—Isa. lxiii, 16.

I am a Father to Israel.—Jerem. xxxi, 9.

Have we not all one Father?—Mal. ii, 10.

Ye are sons of the Lord your God.—Deut. xiv, 1.

Israel is My son.—Exod. iv, 22.

5. Cast thy burden upon the Lord and He will sustain thee.—Ps. lv, 22

Commit thy works unto the Lord.—Prov. xvi, 3.

6. Unto Thee, O Lord, do I lift up my soul.—Ps. xxv, 1.

Let us lift up our heart when we lift up our hands unto God in heaven.—Lam. iii, 41.

When I remember these things, I pour out my soul in me.—Ps. xlii, 4.

Trust in the Lord at all times, ye people who pour out your hearts before Him. God is a refuge for us.—Psalm lxii, 8.

Teach me Thy ways. I would walk in Thy truth. Make my heart one to reverence Thy name.—Ps. lxxxvi, 11.

7. I will surely hear their cry.—Exod. xxii, 23.

And it shall come to pass, when he crieth unto Me, that I will hear, for I am gracious.—Exod. xxii, 27.

When you spread forth your hands, I will hide mine eyes from you; yea, when you multiply prayers I will not hear; your hands are full of blood.—Isa. I, 15.

He will be very gracious unto thee at the voice of thy cry; when He will hear it, He will answer thee.—Isa. xxx, 19.

Then thou shalt call, and the Lord will answer; thou shalt cry, and He will say, Behold I am here.—Isa. lviii, 9.

Thou that hearest prayer, unto Thee all flesh come.—Psalm lv, 2.

He heareth the prayer of the righteous.—Prov. xv, 29. c.f. Psalm xxxiv, 17.

If thou seek Him, He will be found of thee.—1 Chron. xxviii, 9.

9. Evening, morn and at noon will I pray and cry aloud, and He will hear my voice.—Ps. lv, 17.

And Daniel, his windows being open in his chamber towards Jerusalem, kneeled upon his knees, three times a day, and prayed, and gave thanks before his God, as he did aforetime.—Dan. vi, 10.

To declare Thy loving kindness in the morning and Thy faithfulness every night.—Ps. xcii, 2.

10. In my distress I cried unto the Lord and He heard me. Ps. cxx, 1.

11. In every place where I make my name to be remembered, I will come to thee and bless thee.—Exod. xx, 24.

12. And it came to pass, that every one who sought the Lord, went forth unto the tabernacle of the congregation.—Exod. xxxiii, 7.

I pour out my soul within me.—Ps. xlii, 4.

13. Behold here am I, let the Lord do to me as seemeth good unto Him.—2 Sam. xv, 26.

It is the Lord, let Him do what seemeth Him best.—1 Sam. iii, 18.

The Lord gave, the Lord hath taken away, blessed be the name of the Lord.—Job i, 21.

17. The Lord is nigh unto all who call upon Him, to all who call upon Him in truth.—Ps. cxlv, 18.

19. The Lord will receive my prayer.—Ps. vi, 9.

But as for me, my prayer is unto Thee, O Lord, in an acceptable time; O God, in the multitude of Thy mercies, answer me in the truth of Thy salvation.—Ps. lxix, 13.

21. What is the hope of the hypocrite? Will God hear his cry when trouble cometh upon him?—Job xxvii, 8, 9.

The sacrifice of the wicked is an abomination unto the Lord, but the prayer of the upright is His delight.—Prov. xv, 8.

22. Your new moons and your appointed feasts My soul hateth. I am weary to bear them.—Isa. i, 14.

When ye spread forth your hands, I will hide Mine eyes from you: yea, when ye make many prayers, I will not hear; your hands are full of blood.—Isa. i, 15.

25. Thine eyes are too pure to behold evil. Thou canst not look upon iniquity.—Hab. i, 13.

37

THE SIXTH CREED.

**I believe with a perfect faith that
all of the words of the prophets are true.**

1. All the messages of God given to us in the Bible by the prophets are true. Their words are the actual messages of God and must be so respected.
2. The Prophets were men or women who foretold to Israel, to certain other nations, and to humanity in general, what was going to happen.
3. The prophets also preached right conduct.
4. Schools for the training of prophets were established by Samuel. The students were called B'nè Ha-nebiim—sons or disciples of the prophets.
*5. The Hebrew for prophet is Nabi, feminine Nebiah.
6. It also means anyone who combined eloquence, music or poetry, etc., with reverence for God and righteous thought, word and act.
7. The prophets, usually known by that name, were prayerful men. It was the habit of prayer, or spiritual communion with God, and constant meditation upon His works and ways, combined with right conduct, that qualified the inspired men and women of the Bible to receive Divine inspiration or Divine messages. Just as physical and mental exercise result in greater physical and mental development, and consequently greater physical and mental possibilities, so spiritual exercises result in greater spiritual development, and consequently greater spiritual possibilities.
8. Prophecy, therefore, means that degree of spiritual development through which we can hear the Word of God, perceive spiritual Light, feel the Divine impulse, and be conscious of the workings of the Divine mind upon our own.
9. The Divine Impulse, once received, is irresistible. The inspired cannot help but speak.

10. The ideals and admonitions of our prophets were derived through the Spiritual Light, Divine Impulse or Mind. They attained the power to perceive them by reason of their spiritual development. The actual perception was permitted only in dreams or visions. This last fact explains all the supernatural occurrences described by them.

11. Among the ideals of our prophets are:

The Fatherhood of God.
The Brotherhood of Man, or Universal Brotherhood.
The Kingdom of God on earth, sometimes called the Kingdom of
  Heaven, or the New Heavens and the New Earth.
All nations to know and serve the one only God.
The Reign of Righteousness on Earth.
Universal Peace or Arbitration instead Of War.
Universal Happiness, or Earth being filled with the glory of the Lord.

12. All humanity owes a debt of respect and gratitude to them for preaching such ideals.

13. And we Hebrews owe them an additional debt when we remember how some of our prophets suffered insult, imprisonment, banishment and even death because of their brave speeches to save our ancestors from sin and penalty.

BIBLE QUOTATIONS.

2. New things do I declare; before they spring forth I tell you of them.—Isa. xlii, 9.

3. Cry aloud, spare not, lift up thy voice like a trumpet, and show My people their transgressions, and the house of Jacob their sins.—Isa. lviii, 1.

5. And they went to Huldah, the prophetess.—2 Kings, xxxii, 14.

6. And Miriam, the prophetess, the sister of Aaron, took a timbrel in her hand * * * * * and answered, Sing to the Lord, for He hath triumphed gloriously; the horse and his rider hath He cast in the sea.—Exod. xv, 20-21.

And Deborah, a prophetess, the wife of Lapidoth, judged Israel at that time. —Judges iv, 4.

7. And Moses said unto them, stand, and I will hear what the Lord will command concerning you.—Num. ix, 8.

8. And the Lord said unto Moses, Take thee Joshua, the son of Nun, a man in whom is the spirit.— xxvii, 18.

The spirit of the Lord God is upon me, because the Lord hath appointed me to preach good tidings to the meek, He hath sent me to bind up his brokenhearted * * * * * to comfort all that mourn.—Isa. lxi, 1-2.

And the spirit entered into me when he spake unto me.—Ezek. ii, 2; iii, 24.

9. The Lord God speaketh, who can but prophesy?—Amos iii, 8.

Then I said, I will not make mention of Him, nor speak any more in His name. But His word was in mine heart as a burning fire shut up in my bones, and I was weary with forbearing, and I could not stay.—Jer. xx, 9.

And God gave him another heart * * * * * and behold, a company of prophets met him: and the spirit of God came upon him, and he prophesied among them.—I Sam. x, 9-10.

10. And He said, hear now My words; if there be a prophet among you, I, the Lord, will make Myself known unto him in a vision, and will speak unto him in a dream.—Num. xii, 6.

For God will not do anything without He hath revealed His purpose by His servants, the prophets.—Amos iii, 7.

I have spoken by the prophets and I have multiplied visions, and used similitudes by the ministry of the prophets.—Hos. xii, 10.

13. And there was also a man that prophesied in the name of the Lord, Uriyah * * * * * And they fetched him forth out of Egypt, and brought him unto Jehoiakim the King, who slew him with the sword, and cast his dead body into the graves of the common people.—Jerem. xxvi, 20-23.

And the princes were wroth with Jeremiah, and smote him and put him in prison.—Jerem. xxxvii, 15.

* * * * * And he remained there many days.—16.

Then Zedekiah sent and took him out * * * * * and commanded that they should commit him unto the court of the prison * * * * * —21.

And the princes said unto the king, we beseech thee, let this man be put to death.—xxxviii, 4.

Then they cast him in the dungeon * * * * * and he sank in the mire.—6.

And Evedmelech the Ethiopian, * * * * * spake to the king * * * * * —7-8.

And the king commanded saying, Take thirty men with thee and take up Jeremiah the prophet out of the dungeon before he die.—10.

So they drew him up with cords * * * * * and he remained in the court of the prison.—13.

And Amaziah, priest of Bethel, said to Amos, O thou seer, go flee thee away into the land of Judah.—Amos vii, 12.

But they refused to hearken, and pulled away the shoulder, and stopped their ears, that they should not hear.—Zech. vii, 11.

Yea, they made their hearts as an adamant stone lest they should hear the law, and the words which the Lord of Hosts hath sent by His spirit by the former prophets.—12.

38

THE SEVENTH CREED.

I believe with a perfect faith that the prophecies of Moses our Master, peace be to him, are true; and that he is the chief of all the prophets before and after him.

1. All that Moses prophesied about Israel has come to pass; his prophesies were therefore true.
2. The title, "our Master," is one of great respect. It was applied in Bible days (Adon) to God, to kings, prophets, leaders, etc., just as Lord is applied today also to certain noblemen. It was applied in later days to teachers (rabbi or ribi).
3. Moses is the greatest of all our teachers. He devoted his life to serve his people.
4. Because of his goodness he received divine messages while awake, in full possession of his faculties; not in visions, and not by parables.
   All other prophets who received messages received them in a vision or dream.
   *5. This explains the many strange events described by the prophets. They were all seen in a vision or dream.
6. There are other prophets mentioned in the Bible besides those whose books or utterances have been preserved.
7. There were many men who pretended to be prophets. The true test was a righteous life, obedience to God's Laws, and saying nothing in opposition to His Law and His announcements.
8. The Bible says, "God spoke to Moses face to face" (Exod. xxxiii, 11); "Mouth to mouth I will speak with him" (Num. xii, 8). These expressions are

Hebrew idioms, meaning one directly to the other, "As one speaketh to a friend" (Exod. xxxiii, 11.)

9. No mortal can see God's presence, God is incorporeal.

10. Our gratitude to Moses for all he did for us, for all he has taught us, can only be proved to be real by our living lives in accordance with "the law which Moses commanded us, the inheritance of the congregation of Jacob."

BIBLE QUOTATIONS.

1. There failed not aught of any good thing which the Lord hath spoken unto the house of Israel; all came to pass.—Joshua xxi, 45.

Blessed be the Lord who hath given rest unto His people Israel, according to all that He promised: there hath not failed one word of all His good promise, which He promised by the hand of Moses, His servant.—1 Kings viii, 56.

2. If I be a master, where is My respect—Mal. i, 6.

Your master, Saul, is dead.—2 Sam. ii, 7.

Thus shall ye say to your master.—2 Kings xix, 6; Isa. xxxvii, 6.

Alas, master, it was borrowed.—2 Kings vi, 5.

And Chananiah, the master of the song, was with the singers.—1 Chron. xv, 27.

3. And there arose not again a prophet in Israel like unto Moses whom the Lord knew face to face.—Deut. xxxiv, 10.

4. And He said, Hear now My words; if there be a prophet among you, I the Lord will make Myself known unto him in a vision and will speak to him in a dream.

My servant Moses is not so; in all My house he is faithful.

With him will I speak mouth to mouth, and also by vision and not in dark speeches; and the similitude of the Lord he shall behold.—Num. xii, 6-8.

4. After these things, the word of the Lord came unto Abram in a vision, saying, Fear not, Abram; I am thy shield, and thy exceeding great reward.—Gen. xv, 1.

And the Lord appeared unto him (Isaac) the same night, and said, I am the God of Abraham thy father. Fear not, for I am with thee, and will bless thee.—Gen. xxvi, 24.

And Jacob lay down in that place to sleep; and he dreamed, and behold, a ladder set upon the earth and the Lord said, I am the Lord God of Abraham thy father and the God of Israel * * * * * And, behold, I am with thee, and will keep thee in all places whither thou goest * * * * —Gen, xxviii, 11-15.

And it came to pass that night, that the word of the Lord came unto Nathan.—2 Sam. vii, 4.

And Samuel feared to show Eli the vision.—1 Sam. iii, 15.

The vision of Isaiah.—Isa. i, 1.

And the Lord answered me, and said, Write the vision, and make it plain upon tablets, that he who runs may read.—Hab. ii, 2.

6. The prophet Ahijah, the Shilonite.—1 Kings, xi, 29.

Now there dwelt an aged prophet in Bethel.—1 Kings, xiii, 11.

Jehu the prophet.—1 Kings xvi, 12.

Then said Elijah, unto the people, I, even I only, remain a prophet of the Lord, but Baal's prophets are four hundred and fifty men.—1 Kings, xviii, 22.

Elisha, the prophet that is in Israel, telleth the king of Israel the words that thou speakest *even* in thy bedchamber.—2 Kings vi, 12.

Then came Shemaiah the prophet.—2 Chron. xii, 5.

The record of the prophet, Iddo.—2 Chron. xiii, 22.

And the spirit of God came upon Azariah the son of Oded.

And he went out to meet Asa, and said unto him, Hear ye me, Asa, and all Judah and Benjamin; the Lord is with you, while ye be with Him; and if ye ask Him, He will be found of you; but if ye forsake Him, He will forsake you * * * * * Be strong, therefore, and let not your hand be weak: for your work will be rewarded.

And when Asa heard these words, and the prophecy of Oded the prophet, he took courage.—2 Chron. xv, 1-8.

And Jehoshaphat said, Is there not here a prophet?

And the king of Israel said, there is yet one man, Michaiah the son of Imlah by whom we may enquire of the Lord.—I. Kings xxii, 7, 8.

7. Then the king of Israel gathered the prophets together, about four hundred men, and said unto them, shall I go against Ramoth-Gilead or shall I forbear?

And they said, go up, for the Lord shall deliver it into the hand of the king. —1 Kings xxii, 6.

Then said the prophet Jeremiah unto Hananiah the prophet, Hear now, O Hananiah, the Lord hath not sent thee; but thou makest this people to trust in a lie.—Jerem. xxviii, 15.

9. And He said, thou canst not see My face; for there shall no man see My face and live.—Exod. xxxiii, 20.

10. And this is the law which Moses set before the children of Israel.—Deut. iv, 44.

39

THE EIGHTH CREED.

I believe with a perfect faith that the Law which at present is in our possession is the same that was given to Moses our Master, may his soul rest in peace.

1. The Torah, or Law of Moses, as we have it, contains the messages which God gave to Moses.
2. These messages have been preserved all these centuries by the care of our scribes, or writers, our rabbis and other learned and pious men.
3. We must prevent any alteration of the text of the Law.
*4. We know, by actual count, how many sentences, words and letters are in each of the five books of the Torah. We know also how many times each letter is used. We reproduce in every copy the enlarged and reduced letters. A scroll of the Torah found incorrect is not used in public worship by strict congregations until corrected. These are all precautions adopted to secure correctness in the text.
5. The Law of Moses is referred to in almost every other book of the Bible, showing that it was well known to the Hebrews in all ages.
6. The Torah is the basis of our religion. All its commands are binding upon us in whatever land we live, except those which Moses himself expressly states are to be observed in Palestine only, such as those which refer to political life, and to sacrificial or Temple worship in Jerusalem.
7. The latter cannot be observed because we are no longer an independent nation and have neither priesthood nor sacrificial worship.

BIBLE QUOTATIONS.

1. And this is the law which Moses set before the children of Israel.

These are the testimonies and the statutes and the judgments which Moses spake unto the children of Israel after they came forth out of Egypt.—Deut. iv, 44, 45.

2. The families of the scribes which dwelt at Jabez * * * * * —1 Chron. ii, 55.

3. Ye shall not add unto the word which I command you, neither shall ye diminish aught from it, that ye may keep the commandments of the Lord your God which I command you.—Deut. iv, 2.

What thing soever I command you, observe to do it; thou shalt not add thereto, nor diminish from it.—Deut. xii, 32.

5. Compare Joshua viii, 30-35, with Deuteronomy xxvii, 1-8.

But the children of the murderers he (King Amaziah) slew not; according unto that which is written in the book of the law of Moses, wherein the Lord commanded, saying the fathers shall not be put to death for the children, nor the children be put to death for the fathers; but every man shall be put to death for his own sin.—2 Kings xiv, 6. [The command referred to is found only in Deuteronomy, the fifth book of the law of Moses. Moses died 641 years before this king.]

And like him (Josiah) was there no king before him that turned to the Lord with all his heart, with all his soul, and with all his might, according to all the law of Moses; neither after him arose there any like him.—2 Kings xxiii, 25.

Remember ye the law of Moses My servant, which I commanded to him in Horeb for all Israel, the statutes and judgments.—Mal. iv, 4.

Moses died A. M. 2488.
Joshua died A. M. 2516.
Amaziah died A. M. 3129.
Josiah died A. M. 3329.
Malachi lived circa 3409 A. M.

40

THE NINTH CREED.

I believe with a perfect faith in this Law will never be changed, neither will there be another Law from the Creator, blessed be His name

1. Our Torah, our Bible, may not be set aside for the so-called New Testament of the Christians, nor for the Koran of the Mohammedans, nor for any of the so-called sacred books of other religions, nor for any of the religious or ethical movements of our own day.
2. Our Torah was given us by God. He does not change. And His word stands for ever.
3. We must be loyal to the Torah, as a soldier is to his flag.
*4. It is because we believe that our Law never was and never is to be changed, that we reject Christianity.
5. Christianity is the religion founded on the so-called New Testament.

For reasons why we Hebrews reject Christianity see chapter LI.—The attitude of Judaism to Christianity.

BIBLE QUOTATIONS.

2. The word of our Lord shall stand for ever.—Isa. xl, 8.
I am the Lord. I change not.—Mal. iii, 6.
3. Who is on the Lord's side? *let him come* to me.—Exod. xxxii, 26.
How long halt ye between two opinions?—1 Kings xviii, 21.
4. Whatsoever I command you, observe to do it: thou shalt not add thereto, nor diminish from it.—Deut. xii, 32.

41

THE TENTH CREED.

I believe with a perfect faith that the Creator, blessed be His name, knows all the thoughts and actions of man, as it is said, "He who formeth their hearts alike understandeth all their deeds." (Psalm xxxiii, 15.)

1. From this we learn that God is all-knowing, or omniscient.
2. Whatever we do or say or think, God knows. Our conduct should be regulated accordingly.
3. It is useless for us to try and deceive God by false excuses. God knows our thoughts.
*4. God knows what conduct should be expected of us by reason of our intelligence or education or environment.
5. The greater our intelligence, the better our education, the more enlightened our environment, the higher are the ideals of conduct expected from us by God and by man.
6. God has given us the power of discerning between right and wrong. He knows that we possess that power. Therefore we must use it rightly and wisely.

BIBLE QUOTATIONS.

1. For the Lord is a God of knowledge, and by Him actions are weighed.—1 Sam. ii, 3.

Can any one hide himself in secret places, that I shall not see him? saith the Lord. Do not I fill the heaven and the earth, saith the Lord. Jerem. xxiii, 24.

For His eyes are upon the ways of man, and He seeth all his doings.—Job xxxiv, 21.

2. He who formeth their hearts alike, understandeth all their deeds.—Ps. xxxiii, 15.

He knoweth their works.—Job xxxiv, 25.

O Lord, Thou searchest me, and Thou knowest.—Ps. cxxxix, 1.

Thou knowest my downsitting, and mine uprising. Thou understandest my thoughts afar off.—Ps. cxxxix, 2.

Thou art acquainted with all my ways.—Ps. cxxxix, 3.

For there is not a word on my tongue, but lo, O Lord, Thou knowest it altogether.—Ps. cxxxix, 4.

The Lord knoweth the thoughts of man.—Ps. xciv, 11.

He knoweth the secrets of the heart.—Ps. xliv, 21.

And thine ears shall hear a word behind thee, saying, This is the way, walk ye in it, when ye turn to the right hand and when ye turn to the left.—Isa. xxx, 21.

3. The house of Israel compasseth Me with deceit—Hos. xi, 12.

He that planted the ear, shall He not hear? He that formed the eye, shall He not see?—Ps. xciv, 9.

I, the Lord, search the heart.—Jerem. xvii, 10.

4. For God shall bring every work into judgment with every secret thing, whether it be good or whether it be evil.—Eccles. xii, 14.

5. And the Lord spake unto Moses and Aaron, Because ye believed Me not, to sanctify Me in the eyes of the children of Israel, therefore ye shall not bring this congregation unto the land which I have given them.—Numbers xx, 12.

6. I call heaven and earth to witness against you this day, that I have set before you the life and the death, the blessing and the blighting: therefore choose life that thou and thy seed may live.—Deut. xxx, 19.

For the ear triest words as the mouth tasteth meat. Let us choose to us judgment: let us know among ourselves what is good.—Job xxxiv, 3, 4.

THE ELEVENTH CREED.

I believe with a perfect faith that the Creator, blessed be His name, rewards those who keep His commandments, and punishes those who transgress them.

1. Virtue brings its own reward. Sin brings its own punishment.
2. God does not punish in the sense of vengeance but only for correction, in order that we shall forsake our sins and lead better lives.
3. God rewards and corrects sometimes in this life and sometimes in future life.
4. God sends the reward or penalty when He thinks best.
5. Therefore we must not wonder if a righteous man remains long unrewarded or if a wicked man remains long uncorrected.
*6. Suffering is not sent to us only for punishment of sin. It is often sent to arouse us to better and nobler lives, to educate us to higher ideals, to lead us nearer to God.
*7. God made us. In everyone there is some good. God will in His own way develop that good in this or in future life, until the good shall overcome the evil.
8. God has given us Free-will, to choose between good and evil, or right and wrong.
9. If we were destined to do right or wrong and did not have the power to choose, there would be no merit in doing the right, and we could not be justly punished for doing the wrong.
10. We Hebrews therefore do not believe in Predestination.
11. Nor do we believe in anyone suffering in order that any sinner may be saved from the results of his own sin. The soul that sins must suffer.

12. We Hebrews do not believe in vicarious atonement.

13. Only by repentance, or sorrow for our sin, and by amendment of our conduct, can we be saved from the full penalty of our transgressions

14. Some of the penalty we cannot escape. The very remorse is itself a pain or penalty. The loss of our own self-respect, the loss of the respect of others; the shame which our sin causes our families; the consciousness that we have offended God who loves us, all these are some of the penalties or punishments for sin committed.

15. God's punishment is like the good physician's medicine or the good surgeon's knife. The medicine may be bitter and the knife may seem cruel. But they are meant to heal us and save our lives.

16. God does not punish for ever.

17. We Hebrews therefore do not believe in Eternal Punishment.

18. "As a father corrects his child, so God corrects us." (Deut. viii. 5.) His punishment or correction is only fatherly; it is to reform our conduct and to make us better men and women.

19. The greatest reward, the greatest happiness in this life is the consciousness of being at peace with God, or "at one" with Him. Our sins make us at variance with Him until we atone for them. Hence atonement really means at-one-ment, or being again "at one" with God.

20. The greatest reward, the greatest happiness that we can have in future life is a higher spiritual development through which we will be worthy of higher duties and responsibilities, the discharge of which will be yet more pleasing to our God.

BIBLE QUOTATIONS.

1. Know that your sin will find you out.—Num. xxxii, 23.

I the Lord, search the heart, I try the reins, even to give man according to his ways and according to the fruit of his doings.—Jer. xvii, 10.

Say ye unto the righteous that it shall be well with him for they shall eat the fruit of their doings. Woe unto the wicked! it shall be ill with him, for the recompense of his hands shall be done to him.—Isa. iii, 10, 11.

Great in counsel and mighty in doing, for Thine eyes are open upon all the ways of the sons of men, to give every one according to his ways, and according to the fruit of his doing.—Jerem. xxxii, 19.

Doth not He that pondereth the heart consider, and He that keepeth the soul, doth not He know, and shall He not render to every man according to his works?—Prov. xxiv, 12.

2. Have I any pleasure at all that the wicked should die? saith the Lord God: and not that he should return from his ways and live?—Ezek. xviii, 23.

Let the wicked forsake his way, and the man of iniquity his thoughts, and let him return unto the Lord, and He will have mercy upon him, and to our God, and He will abundantly pardon.—Is. lv, 7.

3. God will bring every work into judgment, with every secret thing, whether it be good or whether it be evil.—Eccles. xii, 14.

I will not justify the wicked.—Exod. xxiii, 7.

I will be gracious to whom I will be gracious, and I will show mercy on whom I will show mercy.—Exod. xxxiii, 19.

5. Until the time that His word came, the word of the Lord tried him.—Psalm cv, 19.

I said in mine heart, God shall judge the righteous and the wicked, for there is time there for every purpose and for every work.—Eccles. iii, 17.

There is a just man that perisheth in his righteousness, and there is a wicked man that prolongeth his life in his wickedness.—Eccles. vii, 15.

Because sentence against an evil work is not executed speedily, therefore the heart of the sons of men is fully set in them to do evil.—Eccles. viii, 11.

Though a sinner do evil a hundred times, and his days be prolonged, yet surely I know that it shall be well with them that fear God, who fear before Him.—Eccles. viii, 12.

But it shall not be well with the wicked, neither shall he prolong his days, *which are* as a shadow, because he feareth not before God.—Eccles. viii, 13.

Many are the afflictions of the righteous, but the Lord delivereth them out of them all.—Psalm xxxiv, 19.

Fret not thyself because of evil doers, neither be thou envious against the workers of iniquity.—Psalm xxxvii, 1.

For they shall soon be cut down like grass, and wither as the green herb.—Psalm xxxvii, 2.

For evil doers shall be cut off; but those that wait upon the Lord shall inherit the earth.—Psalm xxxvii, 9.

For yet a little while, and the wicked shall not be.—Psalm xxxvii, 10.

6. In the days of adversity consider.—Eccles. vii, 14.

Let us search and try our ways, and turn again to the Lord.—Lamen. iii, 40.

Weeping may endure for the night, but joy cometh in the morning.—Psalm xxx, 5.

The rain concealeth blessings.—Psalm lxxxiv, 6.

They that sow in tears shall reap in joy.—Psalm cxxvi, 5.

I know, O Lord, that Thy judgments are right, and that Thou in faithfulness hast afflicted me.—Psalm cxix, 75.

7. And God created man . . . . and God saw everything that He had made, and, behold, it was very good.—Gen. i, 27-31.

8. See, I set before thee this day life and good and death and evil.—Deut. xxx, 15.

I call heaven and earth to witness this day against you, that I set before you life and death, blessing and blighting—therefore choose life that both thou and thy children may live.—Deut. xxx, 19.

9. Shall not the Judge of all the earth do right?—Gen. xviii, 25.

A God of Truth and without iniquity, just and upright is He.—Deut. xxxii, 4.

Righteous art Thou, O Lord, and upright are all Thy judgments.—Psalm cxix, 137.

The Lord is righteous in all His ways, and holy in all His works.—Psalm cxlv, 17.

13. When thou art in tribulation, and all these things come upon thee, even in the latter days, if them turn to the Lord thy God, and shalt be obedient unto His voice (for the Lord thy God is a merciful God), He will not forsake thee, neither destroy thee, nor forget the covenant of thy fathers which He promised unto them.—Deut. iv, 30, 31.

Let the wicked forsake his way, and the man of iniquity his thoughts; and let him return unto the Lord, and He will have mercy upon him, and unto our God, for He will abundantly pardon.—Isa. lv, 7.

He, that covereth his sins shall not prosper: but whoso confesseth and forsaketh them shall have mercy.—Prov. xxviii, 13.

16. For I will not contend for ever, neither will I be always wroth; for the spirit would fail before Me, and the souls which I have made.—Isa. lvii, 16.

I am merciful, saith the Lord, I will not keep *anger* for ever.—Jer. iii, 12.

He retaineth not His anger for ever, because He delighteth in mercy.—Micah vii, 18.

The Lord is merciful and gracious, slow to anger and plenteous in mercy.

He will not always chide; neither will He keep *His anger* for ever.

He dealeth not with us according to our sins; nor rewardeth us according to our iniquities.

For as the heaven is high above the earth, so great is His mercy toward them that fear Him.

As the East is far from the West, so doth He remove our transgressions from us. Like as a father pitieth his children, so the Lord pitieth them that fear Him. For He knoweth of what we are formed; it is remembered that we are but dust.—Psalm ciii, 8-14.

18. As a man chasteneth his son, so the Lord chasteneth thee.—Deut. viii, 5.

Happy is the man whom Thou chasteneth, O Lord, and from Thy Law wilt Thou teach him.—Psalm xciv, 12.

Behold, happy is the man whom God correcteth; therefore despise thou not the chastening of the Almighty.—Job v, 17.

19. May the Lord lift up His countenance upon thee and give thee peace.—Numbers vi, 26.

He shall make peace with Me.—Isa. xxvii, 5.

Peace, peace, to him that is far off, and to him that is near, saith the Lord, and I will heal him.—Isa. lvii, 19.

Ye shall have peace.—Jerem. iv, 10.

20. For since the beginning of the world men have not heard, neither hath the eye seen, O God, beside Thee, what He hath prepared for him that waiteth for Him.—Isa. lxiv, 4.

O, how great is Thy goodness, which Thou hast wrought for them that trust in Thee before the sons of men.—Psalm xxxi, 19.

43

THE TWELFTH CREED.

I believe with a perfect faith in the coming of the Messiah; and though he tarry, yet will I daily wait for his coming.

1. All Hebrews believe in a Messianic Era.
2. The Messianic Era is a name given to the time when Universal Peace, Universal Brotherhood and Universal Happiness will be established on earth.
3. This era is also known by various names, e.g., the establishment of God's Kingdom on Earth, the Kingdom of God, the Kingdom of Heaven, the New Heaven and the New Earth, the Era of Peace and Goodwill, etc.
*4. We can only prepare for it by living righteous lives and so setting a proper example.
5. This era will be brought about by the Hebrews, We call the Hebrews, therefore, the Messianic people.
6. The great mass of the Hebrews believe in a personal Messiah, a man of the line of David, and who will be known by his "wisdom and understanding, his counsel and power, his knowledge of the Lord, and his reverence for Him."
7. Messiah means "anointed." A king, in ancient times was anointed when first he assumed his duties, or was selected.
8. The Messiah will be king in the sense of the Hebrew word, which means a "leader," or "guide," or "captain," the head of our government so far as government is required for law and order.
9. He will be identified with the restoration of Palestine to the Hebrews, and the reconstruction of the Hebrew nation, when "the Lord will set His hand again the second time to recover the remnant of his people," "will assemble the outcasts of Israel and gather together the dispersed of Judah from the four corners of the earth" (Isa. xi, 11-12).

10. The reconstructed Hebrew nation will be a spiritual and not a political power, in the modern sense of the term.

11. That is, it will not have army or navy, colonies, protectorates, foreign possessions of any kind, since its boundaries are unchangeably fixed by the Bible.

12. Hebrews living in countries outside of Palestine will owe allegiance in temporal affairs to the country of their birth or adoption, but will be guided spiritually from Jerusalem, just as Catholics give their allegiance to the country of birth or adoption in temporal affairs, but are at the same time guided spiritually by Rome or the Vatican.

13. Hebrews are to be living examples of good citizenship, true manhood and womanhood, in whatever country they live.

14. Only thus can we Hebrews fulfil our mission to be a kingdom of priests and a consecrated nation. As priests we must live among those whom we are to instruct by word and example. As a nation consecrated to God's service, we must do His work wherever it is is to be done. And that is, in every land.

15. Messiah will be identified with the establishment of God's Kingdom on earth, when wars will cease; and Universal Peace, Universal Brotherhood and Universal Happiness will be instituted.

16. The appearance of Messiah, the construction of Israel's nationality, its power as a spiritual force for the happiness of all mankind, the establishment of Universal Peace, Universal Brotherhood and Universal Happiness, the creation of the Kingdom of God on earth, may all seem humanly impossible. But there was a time when it seemed humanly impossible that a deliverer could appear to our fathers in Egypt, or that the Hebrews could be marched into Palestine successfully against martial opponents, or that a Hebrew nationality could be erected whose political power was little or none, but whose spiritual power through its prophets, its real leaders, is to this day a mighty spiritual force which helps to lift all mankind toward the lofty and noble human ideals above-mentioned.

17. Our duty to-day is to hold up these Messianic ideals of the Kingdom of God; and to preach and practice the ideals of life, private or personal, social or communal, civic or political, in whatever country we live. We are to be, individually and collectively, mankind's quickening influence for good. Thus do we best serve the purpose of God to make earth the scene of human happiness. Thus are we the servants of God, the people of God, the ones "chosen" for this purpose.

18. The Messianic ideal, or the ultimate realization of God's Kingdom on earth, is the only reason for our existence as Hebrews.

19. Our religion therefore consecrates us to service of God and service for God. It keeps us separate from all peoples until all shall recognize the one God, the one Savior, and until all shall worship Him, and only Him, not only by words but by conduct.

20. He has chosen other nations for other purposes. He chose Israel to teach mankind conduct; or, as the Bible phrases it, for His praise, name and glory.

21. Praise, name and glory are evidenced not only by words, but by Conduct.

Even as the true praise, name and glory of a parent are the right conduct of his children, and of a monarch the virtue and obedience of his subjects, so the true praise, name and glory of God, the King of Kings, are the right conduct, virtue and obedience of all His earthly children.

22. The consciousness of the high purpose of Israel among the nations should make every Hebrew loyal to God and His Law.

BIBLE QUOTATIONS.

1. As truly as I live, all the earth shall be filled with the glory of the Lord.—Numbers xiv, 21.

Holy, holy, holy is the Lord of Hosts, the whole earth is full of His glory.—Isa. vi, 3.

For as the earth bringeth forth her bud, and as the garden causeth the things that are sown in it to spring forth, so the Lord God will cause righteousness and praise to spring forth before all the nations.—Isa. lxi, 11.

2. And the result of righteousness shall be peace; and the effect of righteousness quietness and assurance forever.—Isa. xxxii, 17.

And My people shall dwell in a peaceable habitation, and in sure dwellings, and in quiet resting places.—Isa. xxxii, 18.

Glory shall dwell in our land. Mercy and truth are met together; righteousness and peace kiss. Truth shall spring forth out of the earth, and charity shall look down from heaven. Yea, the Lord will give happiness.—Psalm lxxxv, 9-12.

They shall not hurt nor destroy in all My holy mountain. For earth shall be filled with the knowledge of the Lord, as the waters cover the sea.—Isa. xi, 9.

Earth shall be filled with the knowledge of the glory of the Lord, as the waters cover the sea.—Hab. ii, 14.

3. See *quotations to chapter 4.*

4. Thou art My servant, O Israel, by whom I will be glorified.

It is a light thing that thou shouldst be My servant to raise up the tribes of Jacob, and to restore the preserved of Israel, I will also give thee for a light to the Gentiles that thou mayest be My salvation to the end of the earth.—Isa. xlix, 3, 6.

6. And there shall come forth a rod out of the stem of Jesse and a branch shall grow out of his roots.—Isa. xi, 1.

And David My servant, shall be king over them, and they shall all have one shepherd; they shall also walk in My judgments, and observe My statutes and do them.—Ezek. xxxvii, 24.

My servant David shall be their prince for ever,—Ezek. xxxvii, 25.

Thus said the Lord, If ye can break My covenant of the day and My covenant of the night, and that there should not be day and night in their season; Then may also My covenant be broken with David My servant, that he should not have a son to reign upon his throne.—Jerem. xxxiii, 20, 21.

And the Spirit of the Lord shall rest upon him, the spirit of wisdom and understanding, the spirit of counsel and of might, the spirit of knowledge of and reverence of the Lord.—Isa. xi, 2.

7. Then Samuel took the horn of oil, and poured it upon his (Saul's) head, and kissed him and said. Is it not because the Lord hath anointed thee to be captain over His inheritance?—I. Sam. x, 1.

And the Lord said unto Samuel, How long wilt thou mourn for Saul, seeing I have rejected him from reigning over Israel? Fill thine horn with oil, and go, I will send thee to Jesse, the Bethlehemite, for I have provided Me a king among his sons.—I. Sam. xvi, 1.

Then Samuel took the horn of oil, and anointed him (David) in the midst of his brethren; and the spirit of the Lord came upon David from that day forward.—I. Sam. xvi, 13.

I have anointed thee king over Israel.—II. Kings ix, 1-3.

8. We will have a king over us; that our king may judge us, and go out before us, and fight our battles.—I. Sam. viii, 19-20.

9. And in that day there shall be a root of Jesse which shall stand for an ensign of peoples, to it shall the Gentiles seek, and His rest shall be glorious.—Is. xi, 10.

And it shall come to pass in that day . . . . He shall set up an ensign for the nations, and shall assemble the outcasts of Israel and gather together the dispersed of Judah from the four corners of the earth.—Is. xi, 11, 12.

10. They shall sanctify My name and sanctify the Holy One of Jacob, and shall fear the God of Israel.—Is. xxix, 23.

Not by might nor by power, but by My spirit, saith the Lord of Hosts.—Zech. iv, 6.

11. Unto thy seed do I give this land, from the river of Egypt unto the great river, the river Euphrates.—Gen. xv, 18.

From the wilderness and Lebanon, from the river, the river Euphrates, even unto the rear sea, shall be your border.—Deut. xi, 24.

12. Seek ye the peace of the city whither I caused you to be carried away captives, and pray unto the Lord for it: for in the peace thereof ye shall have peace.—Jere. xxix, 7.

From Zion shall go forth Law and the word of the Lord from Jerusalem.—Isa. ii, 3; Mica. iv, 2.

13. And their seed shall be known among the Gentiles, and their offspring among the peoples; all that see them shall acknowledge them that they are the seed which the Lord hath blessed.—Isa. lxi, 9.

14. And ye shall be unto Me a kingdom of priests and a holy nation.—Ex. xix, 6.

Ye shall be named the priests of the Lord; men shall call you the ministers of our God.—Isa. lxi, 6.

15. And the Lord shall be King over all the earth. On that day the Lord will be One, and His name One.—Zech. xiv, 9.

And the glory of the Lord shall be revealed, and all flesh shall see it together, for the mouth of the Lord has spoken.—Isa. xl, 5.

They shall beat their swords into ploughshares, and their spears into pruning hooks; nation shall not lift up sword against nation, neither shall they learn war any more.—Isa. ii, 4.

16. And the Lord said unto Moses, Hath the Lord's hand waxed short? Thou shalt see now whether My word shall come to pass unto thee or not.—Num. xi, 23.

I, the Lord, will hasten it in its time.—Isa. lx, 22.

Is My hand shortened at all, that it cannot redeem? Or have I no power to deliver?—Isa. l, 2.

There is nothing too hard for Thee.—Jere. xxxii, 17.

17. To make known on earth Thy ways, Thy salvation among all nations.—Ps. lxvii, 2.

They shall speak of the glory of Thy kingdom, and talk of Thy might.—Ps. cxlv, 11.

To make known to the sons of men His mighty acts, and the glorious majesty of His Kingdom.—Psalm cxlv, 12.

For Thou art a holy people unto the Lord thy God.—Deut. vii, 6.

I will give thee for a light to the nations, that thou mayest be My salvation unto the ends of the earth.—Isa. xlix, 6.

But thou Israel, art My servant, Jacob whom I have chosen, the seed of Abraham, My friend.—Isa. xli, 8; xlii, 10; xliv, 2. 21; xlv, 4.

18. Be a blessing. (God's first message to Abraham, the first of the Patriarchs.)

In thee shall all families of the earth be blessed.—Gen. xii. 2, 3; xvii, 18; xxii, 18; xxvi, 4.

In order that all the peoples of the earth may know that the Lord is God, there is none else.—1 K. viii, 60. (Solomon, at the dedication of the temple.)

19. And ye shall be holy unto Me, for I, the Lord, am Holy, and I have separated you from other peoples, to be Mine.—Levit. xx, 26.

That all the kingdoms of the earth may know that Thou art the Lord, even Thou only.—Isa. xxxvii, 20.

And the Lord shall be King over the earth; on that day the Lord shall be one, and His name one.—Zech. xiv, 19.

All the nations whom Thou hast made shall come and worship before Thee, O Lord; and shall honor Thy name.—Ps. lxxxvi, 9.

And all flesh shall bless the name of His Holiness forever and ever.—Ps. cxlv, 21.

For then I will turn to the peoples a pure language, that they may all call upon the name of the Lord, to serve Him with one consent.—Zeph. iii, 9.

From Zion shall go forth Law, and the word of the Lord from Jerusalem.—Isa. ii, 3.

Look unto Me, and be saved, all the ends of the earth, for I am God, and there is none else.—Isa. xlv, 22.

The gentiles shall come unto Thee from the ends of the earth.—Jer. xvi, 19.

Now shall He be great unto the ends of the earth.—Mica. v, 4.

O, Let the nations be glad and sing for joy, when Thou wilt judge the Peoples righteously, and the nations on earth Thou wilt guide them.

The peoples shall praise Thee, O God, they shall praise Thee, the peoples, all of them. . . .

All the ends of the earth shall reverence Him.—Ps. lxvii, 7.

20. Blessed be Egypt, My people, and Assyria, the work of My hands, and Israel Mine inheritance.—Isa. xix, 25.

Have not I brought up Israel out of the land of Egypt? And the Philistines from Caphtor, and the Syrians from Kir?—Amos. ix, 7.

The Lord hath anointed thee this day to be His peculiar people, as He hath promised thee, and that thou shouldest keep all His commandments.

And to make thee high *even* above all nations which He hath made, for praise, name and glory, and that thou mayest be a Holy people unto the Lord Thy God, as He hath spoken.—Deut. xxvi, 18, 19.

Ye are My witnesses, sayeth the Lord, and My servant whom I have chosen: that ye may know and believe Me and understand that I am He. Besides Me there is no God formed, neither shall there be any after Me.—Isa. xliii, 10.

Behold, I have given him for a witness to the people, a leader and commander for the people.—Isa. lv, 4.

44

THE THIRTEENTH CREED.

I believe with a perfect faith that there will be a reviving of the dead, at the time when it shall please the Creator, blessed be His name, and exalted be His memorial for ever and ever.

1. We have both a soul and a body. The living are those whose souls and bodies act together. The dead are those whose bodies return to dust and whose souls return to God.
2. The souls thus live again in a new life.
3. This new life is sometimes called "the future state."
4. In the future state we reap the rewards or penalties of our conduct on earth.
5. To do good for the sake of reward in this life or in future state is less worthy than to do good without expectation of reward, but only because God considers it right.
6. To avoid evil for fear of punishment or penalty in this life or in future state is less worthy than to avoid evil, not because we will be rewarded for avoiding it, but because God considers it wrong.
7. Reward and penalty in future state can only be spiritual, for the body ceases to exist.
8. "The reward of the righteous in future life is spiritual happiness, the punishment of the wicked is exclusion from it."
*9. The Bible expression, "the soul being cut off from its people," thus means that in future life, that soul is excluded from the happiness enjoyed by the righteous.
10. Hell, a place of everlasting torment, does not form part of Jewish

doctrine. Sheol Ge-hinnom, are sometimes translated "hell." Sheol means the grave.

11. Ge-hinnom, literally the Valley of Hinnom, was a valley south of Jerusalem, which by reason of its uses became the proverbial expression for any bad place.

12. Eternal Punishment does not form part of Jewish doctrine.

13. God is just, therefore He will not sentence to eternal punishment for sins committed in the comparatively short life on earth.

14. God himself assures us that He is "compassionate and gracious, forbearing and abundant in mercy," and that He will not retain His anger for ever, nor does He contend for ever, nor does He punish us even according to our sins. For these reasons also Eternal Punishment does not form part of Jewish doctrine.

15. Future state for the wicked is therefore corrective. The wicked being "destroyed for ever" doubtless means, therefore, rather that the wickedness will be destroyed or eliminated, and the sinner will be refined from his sin. Not one soul that God has made can be lost for ever. For there is good in every man's soul, since the soul comes from God. That good can be trained and educated to higher and better life, while the sinner "bears the indignation of the Lord, because he has sinned against Him, until He pleads his cause, and executes judgment for him, and He brings him forth to the Light and he beholds His righteousness" (Micah vii, 9).

16. In this life on earth it is the soul which makes us what we are, by its powers of mind or intellect, by its emotions, by its inspirations of love or hatred, self-sacrifice or selfishness, etc.

17. We love our dear ones, and we esteem men and women, not because of their physical form, but because of what their souls make them, because of their characters or natures. The soul is therefore more important than the body.

18. The soul returns to God, and continues to live.

19. The continuance of the soul in future life, the correction of faults, and the strengthening of its nobler powers for higher duties and responsibilities, constitute spiritual existence in future state.

20. What new forms the soul assumes, in place of its bodily form on earth, we cannot know.

21. Science teaches us that there is a constant renewal or transmission of life from form to form, and a gradual development from lower to higher forms of life in the physical world.

22. Law in the physical world indicates similar law in the spiritual world. Therefore we believe that there is in the spiritual world, or in spiritual life, a gradual development to higher conditions of life.

23. Our reason tells us that our intelligence, our emotions, our perceptions of spiritual things, are powers or manifestations of the soul. We may therefore with reason believe that our intelligence, our emotions and our perceptions of spiritual things, developed by our earthly experiences, will be continued in a future Life.

24. Science tells us that our globe is but a part of an ordered Universe, all of whose parts are in wonderful harmony. It is impossible to believe that man, the chief inhabitant of our globe, and endowed with such gifts as Intelligence, Emotion and Spiritual Perceptions, is not in some relation of harmony with sentient creatures as far superior to us in magnitude of powers or functions as the rest of the universe is to our small orb.

25. This harmony must be a spiritual harmony, for our natural parts, our bodies, crumble into the dust.

26. We behold the universe with its bewildering myriads of multitudes of worlds, and every star or planet in every stellar system governed by God's laws, which connect them all. It is impossible that the Lord, the King of that universe, has no plan which brings not only our globe into union with His "Universe-Kingdom," but its inhabitants also. And such union of all the responsible inhabitants of the universe can only be of a spiritual nature.

27. No human intellect can imagine any of the stages of the development of our souls in that spiritual future. And no human intellect can understand the transmission of human souls to other spheres of activity.

28. If the righteous are thus translated to a sphere of higher spiritual possibilities, especially if combined with re-union with those whom they loved on earth, that is of itself Reward.

29. If the wicked fail to reach it, or are deprived of it until further educated, or are cut off from the worthy or from their own loved ones, that is of itself Punishment or Penalty.

30. A blind man can have no conception of the glow of a sunset or sunrise, the wonders of the flecked or heaving ocean, the glories of glen and glade, the beauties of bud and blossom. They are all worlds beyond his ken. What can there not be beyond our ken in worlds beyond the little world we live in, in life far removed from the sphere in which we daily grope?

And granting that we cannot imagine the Future Life, does the fact that we do not know its nature preclude its existence? We do not know the real and full nature of what we call the correlation of forces, the diffusion of gases, gravitation, light, heat, sound, chemical action, electricity, magnetism, molecular action, the countless suns in the firmament, the motions of the myriad myriad stellar systems, and the uncountable phenomena of nature. We cannot explain the mysteries of the 26th chapter of Job. We cannot answer the questions God put to him in that even more wonderful 38th chapter.

But they are all actualities, our consciousness of Which is but dim; facts, our perceptions of which are but dull compared with the possible glories of their full potentialities.

With Job himself, we humbly exclaim, "Lo, these are but whispers of God's ways. And how little a portion is heard of Him! Then the thunder of His power, who can understand?" (Chapter xxvi, 14).

So our emotions, our consciousness of spirituality be it ever so dim; our perception of the powers of the soul, be it ever so dull, may but feebly indicate the full glory of unknown potentialities. With the prophet we exclaim, humbly and reverently, "Men have not heard, nor perceived by the ear, neither hath the eye seen what He hath prepared for him that waiteth for Him!" (Isa. lxiv, 4-5).

With the psalmist we sing, "O, how great is Thy goodness, which Thou hast laid up for them that fear Thee; which Thou hast wrought for them that trust in Thee before the sons of men" (Psalm xxxi, 19).

And the answer to our cry, the echo of our song, is another prophet's words: "I will ransom them from the power of the grave; I will redeem them from death. O death, I will be thy plagues—O grave, I will be thy destruction!" (Hos. xiii, 14).

BIBLE QUOTATIONS.

1. And the Lord God formed man of the dust of the earth, and breathed into his nostrils the breath of life, and man became a living being.—Gen. ii, 7.

2. And thou (Abraham) shalt go to thy fathers in peace.—Gen. xv, 15.

O God, God of the spirits of all flesh.—Num. xvi, 22; xxvii, 16.

I send death, and I make alive.—Deut. xxxii, 39.

The Lord killeth and maketh alive, He bringeth down to the grave and bringeth up.—1 Sam. ii, 6.

Am I God, to kill and make alive again?—2 Kings, v, 7.

Then shall the dust return to the earth as it was and the spirit shall return unto God who gave it.—Ecc. xii, 7.

He will swallow up death forever.—Isa. xxv, 8.

Neither hath the eye seen, O God, besides Thee, what He hath prepared for him that waiteth for Him.—Isa. lxiv, 4.

I will ransom them in the power of the grave, I will redeem them from death: O death, I will be thy plagues! O grave, I will be thy destruction.—Hosea xiii, 14.

Thy dead shall live; with my dead they shall rise; awake and sing ye that dwell in the dust, for thy dew is as the dew of herbs.—Isa. xxvi, 19.

For Thou wilt not leave my soul to the grave neither wilt Thou permit Thy pious to perceive corruption.

Thou wilt show me the path of life, the plenitude of joys before Thee, the happiness at Thy right hand forever.—Ps. xvi, 10-11.

I will behold Thy presence in righteousness.—Ps. xvii, 15.

I shall be satisfied when I awake with Thy likeness.—Ps. xvii, 15.

Into Thy hand I commit my spirit, Thou hast redeemed me, O Lord, God of truth.—Ps. xxxi, 5.

But God will redeem my soul from the power of the grave, when He will take me.—Ps. xlix, 15.

He shall dwell on high: his place of defence shall be the munitions of rocks; bread shall be given him: his waters shall be secured.

Thine eyes shall see the King in His beauty; they shall behold the far-off land.—Isa. xxxiii, 16-17.

For I know my Redeemer liveth, and that He shall stand at the latter day over what is dust, and after my skin hath been thus destroyed, yet in my being shall I see God.

Whom I shall behold for myself, and mine eyes shall behold, and not another, though my reins be consumed within me.—Job xix, 25-27.

Behold, He will slay me, but in Him will I trust; surely I will show my ways in His presence.—Job xiii, 15.

The righteous hath hope in his death.—Prov. xiv, 32.

Also when I walk through the valley of the shadow of death I will fear no evil, for Thou art with me, Thy staff and Thy support, they shall comfort me.—Ps. xxiii, 4.

How great is Thy goodness which Thou hast laid up for those that fear Thee, which Thou hast wrought for those that trust in Thee before the sons of men.—Ps. xxxi, 19.

Mark the perfect man, and behold the upright, for the end of that man is peace.—Ps. xxxvii, 37.

He (the righteous man) shall enter into peace.—Isa. lvii, 2.

How excellent is Thy loving kindness, O God! Therefore the children of men put their trust under the shadow of Thy wings.

They shall be abundantly satisfied with the richness of Thy house, and Thou shalt make them drink of the stream of Thy delights.

For with Thee is the fountain of life; in Thy light shall we see light.—Ps. xxxvi, 7-9 (see Chap. xli, Q. 3, 4, 5).

4. Say to the righteous that they shall have good, for they shall eat the fruit of their doings. Woe unto the wicked, for he shall have evil, for the reward of his hands shall be given to him.—Isa. iii, 10-11.

12. See quotations of No. 14, this chapter.

13. A God of truth, and without iniquity, Just and upright is He.—Deut. xxxii, 4.

A Just God and a Savior.—Isa. xlv, 21.

Shall mortal man be more just than God? Shall a man be more pure than his Maker?—Job iv, 17.

14. The Lord is the Lord God, merciful and gracious, forbearing and abundant in loving-kindness, and truth, keeping loving-kindness for thousands, forgiving iniquity and transgression and sin, but not acquitting the guilty.—Exod. xxxiv, 6, 7.

For I will not contend for ever, neither will I be always wroth, for the Spirit would fail before Me and the souls which I have made.—Isa. lvii, 16.

He retaineth not His anger for ever, because He delighteth in Mercy.—Mich. vii, 18.

For I am merciful, saith the Lord, and I will not keep anger for ever.—Jer. iii, 12.

He will not always chide, neither will He keep His anger for ever.—Ps. ciii, 9.

He doth not deal with us according to our sins, nor requite us according to our iniquities.—Ps. ciii, 10.

For *there is but* a moment in His anger, but *there is* a lifetime in His favor. Weeping may endure for a night, but joy cometh in the morning.—Ps. xxx, 5.

Give thanks unto the Lord, for He is good, for His mercy endureth for ever.—Ps. cxviii, 1.

As the heaven is high above the earth, so doth His loving-kindness exceed toward those that reverence Him. As far as the east is from the west, so far doth He remove our transgressions from us. Like as a father pitieth His children, so the Lord pitieth them that fear Him.—Ps. ciii, 11-13.

15. And God created man . . . Gen. i, 27.

And God saw all that He had made and behold, it was very good.—Gen. i, 31.

And the Lord God breathed into his nostrils the breath of life; and man became a living soul.—Gen. ii, 7.

I will bear the indignation of the Lord, because I have sinned against Him, until He plead my cause, and execute judgment for me; He will bring me forth to the light and I shall behold His righteousness.—Mich. vii, 9.

18. Thou who hast shown me great and sore troubles, shalt quicken me again, and shalt bring me up again from the depths of the earth.—Ps. lxxi, 20.

Thou wilt increase my greatness, and comfort me on every side.—21.

20. The mysteries belong unto the Lord our God. Revelation is ours and our children's for ever, that we may perform all the words of this law.—Deut. xxix, 29.

21. Dead things are re-formed from under the water, and the inhabitants thereof.—Job xxvi, 5.

Thou hidest Thy face, they are troubled; Thou takest away their breath, they die, and return to the dust. Thou sendest forth Thy spirit, they are re-created: and Thou renewest the face of the earth.—Ps. civ, 29, 30.

24. Lift up your eyes on high, and see who hath created these things, who bringeth forth their host by number; to all of them He calleth by name; from a myriad of forces and strength of power not one faileth.—Isa. xl, 26.

He counteth the number of the stars, He calleth them all by name.—Ps. cxlvii, 4.

Job xxxviii beautifully illustrates the law of an ordered universe.

27. For from everlasting, *men* have not heard, nor perceived by the ear, neither hath the eye seen, O God, besides Thee, what He hath prepared for him that waiteth for Him.—Isa. lxiv, 4.

Thou meetest him that rejoiceth and worketh righteousness, those that remember Thee in Thy ways.—Isa. lxiv, 5.

Such knowledge is too wonderful for me; it is high, I cannot attain to it.—Psalm cxxxix, 6.

In His hand is the soul of every living thing and the spirit of all mankind.—Job xii, 10.

LAWS.

45

LAWS OF CONDUCT, OR MORAL LAWS AND ETHICAL TEACHINGS

For method of studying this chapter, see Preface to Teachers.

Besides the conduct-laws taught by the Shema', the Holy Days and Festivals, the Ten Commandments and the Creeds, our religion, as taught to us by the Bible, gives many other moral laws and ethical teachings.

They can best be learned in the words of the Bible.

1. *Affliction*: O Lord, Thou art my refuge in the day of affliction.—Jer. xvi, 19.

2. *Amendment*: Whoso confesseth and forsaketh his sin shall have mercy.—Prov. xxviii, 13.

3. *Anger*: Then said the Lord, Doest thou well to be angry?—Jonah iv, 4.

4. *Anger, retained*: Anger resteth in the bosom of fools.—Eccl. vii, 9.

5. *Anxiety*: Who is there among you who, fearing the Lord, obeying the voice of His servant, walketh in darkness and hath no light? Let him trust in the name of the Lord and rely upon his God.—Isa. l, 10.

6. *Arrogance*: Talk no more so exceeding proudly.—I Sam. ii, 3.

7. *Apathy*: Shall your brethren go to war and shall ye sit here?—Numbers xxxii, 6.

8. *Balances*: A false balance is an abomination to the Lord; but a just weight is His delight.—Prov. xi, 1.

9. *Beauty*: Beauty is vain, but the God-fearing woman is to be praised.—Prov. xxxi, 30.

10. *Behavior*: As a jewel of gold in a swine's nose, so is a beautiful woman without discretion.—Prov. xi, 22.

11. *Benefits from God*: Blessed be the Lord, who daily loadeth us with benefits.—Psalm lxviii, 19.

12. *Blessing of God*: With Thy blessing let the house of Thy servant be blessed for ever.—II Sam. vii, 29.

13. *Blind, The*: Thou shalt not put a stumbling-block before the blind.—Levit. xix, 14.

14. *Bountifulness*: He that hath a bountiful eye shall be blessed.—Prov. xxii, 9.

15. *Boasting*: Let not him that girdeth on *his armor* boast himself as he that putteth it off.—I Kings xx, 11.

16. *Brethren*: Behold, how good and how pleasant it is for brethren to dwell together in unity.—Psalms cxxxiii, 1.

17. *Bribe*: Thou shalt not accept a bribe; for a bribe doth blind the eyes of the wise and pervert the words of the righteous.—Deut. xvi, 19.

18. *Brother*: A brother is born to help in adversity.—Prov. xvii, 17.

19. *Burden*: Cast thy burden on the Lord, He will sustain thee.—Psalms lv, 22.

20. *Business*: Righteousness, righteousness, shalt thou pursue.—Deut. xvi, 20.

21. *Caution*: Boast not thyself of to-morrow, for thou knowest not what a day will bring forth.—Prov. xxvii, 1.

22. *Charity*: Thou shalt open thy hand wide unto thy brother, to thy poor, to thy needy in thy land.—Deut. xv, 11.

23. *Cheerfulness*: A merry heart doeth good like a medicine.—Prov. xvii, 22.

24. *Clean Heart*: Create in me a clean heart, O God, and renew a right spirit within me.—Psalms li, 10.

25. *Communion with God*: Unto Thee, O Lord, I lift up my soul.—Psalm lxxxvi, 4.

26. *Conceit*: Seest thou one wise in his own conceit? There is more hope of a fool than of him.—Prov. xxvi, 12.

27. *Conciliation*: A soft answer turneth away wrath.—Prov. xv, 1.

28. *Conduct*: What doth the Lord require of thee, but to do justly and to love mercy, and to walk humbly with thy God?—Micah vi, 8.

29. *Confession*: My son, give now glory to the Lord God of Israel, and make confession unto Him.—Joshua vii, 19.

30. *Conquest of Sin*: Sin's desire is unto thee; rule thou it.—Gen. iv, 7.

31. *Consecration*: Consecrate yourselves, and be ye holy; for I am the Lord your God.—Levit. xx, 7.

32. *Consolation*: As one whom his mother comforteth, so will I comfort you.—Isa. lxvi, 13.

33. *Contentment*: give me neither poverty nor riches, feed me with the food assigned to me.—Prov. xxx, 8.

34. *Conscience*: And thine ears shall hear a word behind thee saying, This is the way, walk ye in it, when ye turn to the right hand, and when ye turn to the left.—Isa. xxx, 21.

35. *Contrition*: Surely it is meet to be said to God, I have suffered, I will not

offend any more; That which I see not, teach Thou me. If I have done iniquity, I will do so no more.—Job xxxiv, 31-32.

36. *Correction (Friendly)*: Faithful are the words of a friend.—Prov. xxvii, 6.

37. *Covetousness*: Thou shalt not covet.—Exod. xx, 17.

38. *Deaf, The*: Thou shalt not curse the deaf.—Levit. xix, 14.

39. *Deceit*: The Lord abhors the deceitful.—Psalm v,6.

40. *Devotion*: Entreat me not to leave thee, or to return from following after thee: for whither thou goest, I will go, and where thou lodgest, I will lodge; thy people shall be my people, and thy God my God. Where thou diest, will I die, and there will I be buried; The Lord do so to me, and more also, if aught but death part thee and me.—Ruth i, 17.

41. *Discord*: The Lord hateth him that soweth discord among brethren.—Prov. vi, 19.

42. *Dignity*: A little folly in him that is in reputation for wisdom and honor, putteth him in bad odor.—Eccles x, 1.

43. *Dishonesty*: Woe to him who increaseth that which is not his.—Hab. ii, 6.

44. *Door of Hope*: I will appoint the valley of Anxiety to lead to the door of hope.—Hos. ii, 15.

45. *Drawing near to God*: It is good for me to draw near to God.—Psalm lxxiii, 28.

46. *Drunkenness*: Woe unto them that are mighty to drink wine and men of strength to mingle strong drink.—Isa. v, 22.

47. *Duty to the Synagogue or House of God*: We will not forsake the house of our God.—Nehem. x, 39.

48. *Earnestness*: Whatsoever thy hand findeth to do, do it with all thy might.—Eccl. ix, 10.

49. *Endurance*: If thou faint on the day of adversity, thy strength is small.—Prov. xxiv, 10.

50. *Enemy*: If thine enemy be hungry, give him bread to eat; and if he be thirsty, give him water to drink.—Prov. xxv, 21.

51. *Envy*: Envy is the rottenness of the bone.—Prov. xiv, 30.

52. *Evil*: Depart from evil and do good, seek peace and pursue it.—Psalm xxxiv, 14.

53. *Evil Companions*: My son, if sinners entice thee, consent thou not.—Prov. i, 10.

54. *Evil speech*: Keep thy tongue from evil and thy lips from speaking guile.—Psalm xxxiv, 13.

55. *Evil thoughts*: The thoughts of the wicked are an abomination unto the Lord.—Prov. xv, 26.

56. *Examination of Conduct*: Thus saith the Lord of Hosts, Consider your ways.—Haggai i, 5-7.

57. *Exultation*: Rejoice not when thine enemy falleth, and let not thine heart be glad when he stumbleth.—Prov. xxiv, 17.

58. *Faith*: The just shall live by his faith.—Hab. ii, 4.

59. *Faith in God*: Believe in the Lord your God; so shall ye be established; believe His prophets, so shall ye prosper.— II Chron. xx, 20.

60. *Falsehood*: The Lord hateth the lying tongue.—Prov. vi, 17.

61. *Flattery*: Meddle not with him that flattereth with his lips.—Prov. xx, 19.

62. *Forbearance*: The discretion of a man deferreth his anger, and it is his glory to pass over a transgression.—Prov. xix, 11.

63. *Forgiveness*: Forgiveness is with Thee.—Psalm cxxx, 4.

64. *Fool*: A fool uttereth all his mind.—Prov. xxix, 11.

65. *Foolish, The*: Forsake the foolish and live.—Prov. ix, 6.

66. *Fraud*: Thou shalt not defraud thy neighbor.—Lev. xix, 13.

67. *Fretting*: Fret not thyself because of evil doers.— Psalm xxxvii, 1.

68. *Friend*: Thine own friend and thy father's friend, forsake not.—Prov. xxvii, 10.

69. *Generosity*: The righteous giveth and spareth not.—Prov. xxi, 26.

70. *Getting rich quickly*: He that hasteneth to be rich shall not be innocent.—Prov. xxviii, 20.

71. *God, our Benefactor*: All things come of Thee.—I Chron. xxix, 14.

72. *God, our Father*: Thou, O Lord, art our Father.—Isa. lxiii, 16.

73. *God, His Glory*: As truly as I live, all the earth shall be filled with the glory of the Lord.—Num. xiv, 21.

74. *God, His goodness*: The Lord is good, a stronghold in the day of trouble, and He knoweth them that trust in Him.—Nahum i, 7.

75. *God, His justice*: All His ways are just.—Deut. xxxii, 4.

76. *God, love of*: The Lord thy God loveth thee.—Deut. xxiii, 5.

77. *God, love of (for nations)*: Yea, He loveth the peoples.—Deut. xxxiii, 3.

78. *God, love of (for the stranger or non-Hebrew)*: He loveth the stranger.—Deut. x, 18.

79. *God, love of (for all creatures)*: The Lord is good to all, and His tender mercies are over all His works.—Psalm cxlv, 9.

80. *God, Mercy of*: I am merciful, saith the Lord, and I will not keep anger for ever.—Jerem. iii, 12.

81. *God, Might of*: Thine, O Lord, is the greatness and the power and the glory, and the victory and the majesty.—I Chron. xxix, 11.

82. *God, Protection of*: The Eternal God is thy Refuge and underneath are the everlasting arms.—Deut. xxxiii, 27.

83. *God, Providence of*: Thou openest Thy hand, and satisfiest the desire of all living.—Psalm cxlv, 16.

84. *God, Righteousness of*: The righteous Lord is in the midst thereof, He will not do iniquity.—Zeph. iii, 5.

85. *God among us*: Are not these evils come upon us because our God is not among us?—Deut. xxxi, 17.

86. *God with us*: Be strong and of good courage, be not afraid nor be dismayed, for the Lord thy God is with thee whithersoever thou goest.—Joshua i, 9.

87. *God, the Giver of all*: All things come of Thee.—I Chron. xxix, 14.

88. *God and Israel*: Israel is My son, My first-born.—Exod. iv, 22.

89. *God and all nations*: Have we not all One Father? Hath not one God created us?—Mal. ii, 10.

90. *God, trust in*: There is no restraint to the Lord to save by many or by few.—I. Sam. xiv, 6.

91. *Godliness*: Teach me Thy way, O Lord, I will walk in Thy truth; devote my heart solely to revere thy name.—Psalm lxxxvi, 11.

92. *Good*: Trust in the Lord and do good.—Psalm xxxvii, 3.

93. *Gratitude to God*: Honor the Lord with thy substance and with the first fruits of all thine increase.—Prov. iii, 9.

94. *Grudge*: Say not I will do so to him as he hath done to me, I will render to him according to his work.—Prov. xxiv, 29.

95. *Happiness*: Let not the wise man glory in his wisdom, neither let the mighty man glory in his strength; let not the rich man glory in his riches. But let him that glorieth, glory in this; that he understandeth and knoweth Me, that I am the Lord who exerciseth loving kindness, judgment and righteousness on earth; for in these things I delight, saith the Lord.—Jer. ix, 23-24.

96. *Hate*: Thou shalt not hate thy brother in thy heart.—Lev. xix, 17.

97. *Haughtiness*: Pride goeth before destruction and a haughty spirit before a fall.—Prov. xvi, 18.

98. *Holiness of God*: Thou art of too pure eyes to behold evil, and canst not look upon iniquity—Hab. i, 13.

99. *Holiness of Life*: Ye shall be holy, for I, the Lord, your God, am holy.—Levit. xix, 1.

100. *Honor*: My righteousness I hold fast, and will not let it go; my heart shall not reproach me as long as I live.—Job xxvii, 6.

101. *Household*: The good woman looketh well to the ways of her household and eateth not the bread of idleness.—Prov. xxxi, 27.

102. *Hope*: It is good that a man should hope and quietly wait for the salvation of the Lord.—Lam. iii, 26.

103. *Humility*: Seekest thou great things for thyself? Seek them not.—Jer. xlv, 5.

104. *Hypocrisy*: What is the hope of the hypocrite, though he hath gained, when God taketh away his soul?—Job. xxvii, 8.

105. *Idleness*: An idle soul shall suffer hunger.—Prov. xix, 15.

106. *Industry*: In all labor there is profit.—Prov. xiv, 23.

107. *Infidelity*: Woe unto him that striveth with his Maker. . . . Shall the clay say to Him that fashioneth it, what makest thou?—Isa. xlv, 9.

108. *Ingratitude, to God*: Take heed that thou forget not the Lord thy God . . . and when all that thou hast is multiplied . . . that thine heart be lifted up and thou forget the Lord thy God. . . . And thou say in thine heart, my power and the might of mine hand hath gotten me this prosperity. But thou shalt remember the Lord thy God; for it is He that giveth thee power to acquire prosperity.—Deut. viii, 11-18.

109. *Ingratitude, to man*: Whoso repayeth evil for good, evil shall not depart from his house.—Prov. xvii, 13.

110. *Iniquity*: If iniquity be in thy hand, put it far away.—Job xi, 14.

111. *Integrity*: Better is the poor man that walketh in his integrity, than he that is crooked in his ways, though he be rich.—Prov. xxviii, 6.

112. *Irreligion*: Woe to her. . . . She obeyed not the voice; she received not correction; she trusted not in the Lord; she drew not near to her God.—Zeph. iii, 2.

113. *Jealousy*: Jealousy is cruel as the grave; the coals thereof are coals of fire.—Song of Solomon, viii, 6.

114. *Joy in serving God*: Thou servedst not the Lord thy God with joyfulness and with gladness of heart, for the abundance of all.—Deut. xxviii, 47.

115. *Kindness, to man*: Thou shalt love thy neighbor as thyself.—Lev. xix, 18.

116. *Kindness, to strangers*: Thou shalt not oppress a stranger: for ye know the heart of a stranger, seeing ye were strangers in the land of Egypt.—Exod. xxiii, 9.

117. *Kindness, to animals*: Thou shalt not muzzle the ox when he treadeth out the corn.—Deut. xxv, 4.

118. *Kindness, to servants*: The wages of one that is hired shall not abide with thee all night until the morning.—Lev. xix, 13.

119. *Laziness*: Go to the ant, thou sluggard, consider her ways and be wise.—Prov. vi, 6.

120. *Liberality*: He that hath a bountiful eye shall be blessed.—Prov. xxii, 9.

121. *Liberty*: Proclaim Liberty throughout all the land unto all the inhabitants thereof.—Lev. xxv, 10.

122. *Life*: Seek ye Me, and live.—Amos v, 4.

123. *Life, Frailty*: We all do fade as a leaf.—Isa. lxiv, 6.

124. *Light, Divine*: In Thy light shall we see light.—Psalm xxxvi, 9.

125. *Love*: Love is strong as death.—Song of Solomon viii, 6.

126. *Love, of God*: Thou shalt love the Lord thy God with all thy heart, and with all thy soul, and with all thy might.—Deut. vi, 5.

127. *Love, to fellow-beings*: Thou shalt love thy neighbor as thyself.—Lev. xix, 18.

128. *Love, to strangers*: Ye shall love the stranger.—Deut. x, 19.

129. *Loyalty to God*: How long halt ye between two opinions? If the Lord be God, follow Him; but if Baal, then follow him.—I King xviii, 21.

130. *Meekness*: Seek righteousness; seek meekness.—Zeph. ii, 3.

131. *Mischief*: The Lord hateth feet that be swift in running to mischief.—Prov. vi, 18.

132. *Misery*: Thou shalt forget thy misery; thou shalt remember it as waters that have passed away, and thine age shall be clearer than the noonday.—Job xi, 16-17.

133. *Moderation*: If riches increase set not your heart upon them.—Psalm lxii, 10.

134. *Modesty*: Let another man praise thee and not thine own mouth, a stranger and not thine own lips.—Prov. xxvii, 2.

135. *Moral Courage*: Thou shalt in anywise rebuke thy neighbor and not suffer sin through him.—Lev. xix, 17.

136. *Murmuring*: Wherefore doth a living man complain, a man for the punishment of his sins.—Lam. iii, 39.

137. *Nearness to God*: Cast me not away from Thy presence, and take not the spirit of Thy holiness from me.—Psalm li, 11.

138. *Neglect of God's House*: Is it a time for you, O ye, to dwell in your ceiled houses, and this (My) house be waste?—Haggai i, 4.

139. *Obedience to God*: Whatsoever is commanded by the God of Heaven, let it be diligently done.—Ezra vii, 23.

140. *Obedience to government*: Seek ye the peace of the city.—Jerem. xxix, 7.

141. *Officials*: When the righteous are in authority, the people rejoice; but when the wicked bear rule, the people mourn.—Prov. xxix, 2.

142. *Parental Duty*: He will command his children and his household after him, and they shall keep the way of the Lord to do righteousness and judgment.—Gen. xviii, 19.

143. *Partner*: Whoso is partner with a thief, hateth his own soul.—Prov. xxix, 24.

144. *Patriotism*: And he (Mordecai) charged her (Esther) that she should go in unto the king, to make supplication unto him, and to make request before him for her people. And Esther commanded to answer Mordecai. . . . I will go in unto the king, which is not according to the law: and if I perish, I perish.—Esther iv, 8, 15-16.

145. *Penalty*: Say ye to the righteous that it shall be well with them, for they shall eat the fruit of their doings. Woe unto the wicked! it shall be ill with them; for the reward of his hands shall be given him.—Isa. iii, 10-11.

146. *Penitence*: The sacrifices of God are a broken spirit; a broken and a contrite heart, O God, Thou wilt not despise.—Psalm li, 17.

147. *The Poor*: If thy brother become poor, and fallen in poverty with thee, then thou shalt relieve him, yea, though he be a stranger or a sojourner.—Lev. xxv, 35.

148. *Prayer*: And as for me, my prayer is unto Thee, O Lord, in an acceptable time; O God, in the multitude of Thy mercies, answer me in the truth of Thy salvation.—Psalm lxix, 13.

149. *Pride*: Pride goeth before destruction, and an haughty spirit before a fall.—Prov. xvi, 18.

150. *Prudence*: Be not one of them that strike hands, or of them that are sureties for debts. If thou hast nothing to pay, why should he take away thy bed from under thee?—Prov. xxii, 26-27.

151. *Proud Heart*: The pride of thine heart hath deceived thee.—Obad. i, 3.

152. *Proud Look*: The Lord hateth the proud look.—Prov. vi, 17.

153. *Purity*: Embrace purity lest God be angry.—Psalm ii, 11.

154. *Quietness*:—Better is a handful with quietness, than both hands full, with travail and vexation of spirit.—Eccles. iv, 6.

155. *Reaching out Godwards*: My soul thirsteth for God, for the living God.—Psalm xlii, 2.

156. *Recognition of God's goodness*: I am unworthy of any of the loving kindness and of any of the truth which Thou hast shown unto Thy servant.—Gen. xxxii, 10.

157. *Regeneration of Israel*: I will put a new spirit within you; and I will take the stony heart out of their flesh and will give them a heart of flesh.—Ezek. xi, 19.

158. *Regeneration of all mankind*: And it shall come to pass afterward that I will pour out My spirit upon all flesh.—Joel ii, 28.

159. *Religion, a necessity*: Not by bread alone, but by all that proceedeth from the mouth of the Lord, doth man live.—Deut. viii, 3.

160. *Remorse*: Hide Thy face from my sins, and blot out all mine iniquities. Create in me a pure heart, O God; and renew a right spirit within me. Cast me not away from thy presence, and take not Thy holy spirit from me. Restore unto me the joy of thy salvation, and uphold me with Thy free spirit. . . . The sacrifices of God are a broken spirit: a broken and a contrite heart, O God, Thou wilt not despise.—Psalm li, 9-12, 17.

161. *Repentance (See chap. xiv.)*: Break off thy sins by righteousness, and thine iniquities by showing mercy to the poor.—Dan. iv, 27.

162. *Repentant, Israel*: If My people, which are called by My name, shall humble themselves and pray, and seek My face, and turn from their evil ways, then will I hear from heaven, and will forgive their sin.—2 Chron. vii, 14.

163. *Repentant Nations*: If that nation, against which I have pronounced, turn from their evil, I will reconsider the evil I thought to do unto them.—Jerem. xviii, 8.

164. *Resignation*: Behold, here am I, let Him do to me as seemeth good unto Him.—2 Sam. xv, 26.

165. *Rest*: Rest in the Lord, and wait patiently for Him.—Psalm xxxvii, 7.

166. *Retaliation*: Say not I will do so to him as he hath done to me. I will render to the man according to his work.—Prov. xxiv, 29.

167. *Reverence, for God*: Reverence the Lord, and serve Him in sincerity and Truth.—Joshua xxiv, 14.

168. *Reverence for the Aged*: Thou shalt rise up before the hoary head, and thou shalt honor the face of the old.—Lev. xix, 32.

169. *Reverence for the old paths*: Ask for the old paths, wherein is the good way, and walk therein, and ye shall find rest for your souls.—Jerem. vi, 16.

170. *Reverence, for parents*: Ye shall reverence every one his father and his mother.—Lev. xix, 3.

171. *Reverence, for the Sanctuary*: Ye shall reverence My sanctuary.—Lev. xxvi, 2.

172. *Reverence, in Worship*: I will worship toward Thy Holy Temple in reverence of Thee.—Psalm v, 7.

173. *Robbery of God*: Will a man rob God? Yet ye have robbed Me. But ye say, wherein have we robbed Thee? In tithes and in offerings.—Mal. iii, 8.

174. *Riches*: He that getteth riches and not by right, shall leave them in the midst of his days, and at his end shall be a fool.—Jer. xvii, 11.

175. *Right Conduct*: Learn to do well.—Isa. i, 17.

176. *Right-doing*: Do what is right in the eyes of the Lord.—Deut. xxi, 9.

177. *Rulers*: He that ruleth over men must be just, ruling in the fear of God.—2 Sam. xxiii, 3.

178. *Secret faults*: Cleanse Thou me from secret faults.—Psalm xix, 12.

179. *Seeking God*: The hand of our God is upon all them for good that seek Him.—Ezra viii, 22.

180. *Self-control*: He that is slow to anger is better than the mighty; and he that ruleth his spirit is better than he that taketh a city.—Prov. xvi, 32.

181. *Self-Denial*: I will not offer offerings unto the Lord my God of that which doth cost me nothing.—2 Sam. xxiv, 24.

182. *Self-Examination*: Let us search and try our ways, and turn again unto the Lord.—Lam. iii, 40.

183. *Selfishness*: When ye did eat and drink, did ye not eat and drink for yourselves?—Zech. vii, 6.

184. *Self-Righteousness*: All the ways of men are clean in his own eyes, but the Lord weigheth the motives.—Prov. xvi, 2.

185. *Separation of the Hebrews*: I am the Lord your God, who have separated you from other peoples.—Levit. xx, 24.

186. *Silence*: There is a time to keep silence and a time to speak.—Eccl. iii, 7.

187. *Sin*: Know that your sin will find you out.—Numbers xxxii, 23.

188. *Slander*: Guard thy tongue from evil and thy lips from speaking guile.—Psalm xxxiv, 13.

189. *Slothfulness*: The slow man roasteth not that which he took in hunting.—Prov. xii, 27.

190. *Speech*: Take no heed unto all words that are spoken.—Eccl. vii, 21.

191. *Speech, Gentle*: The law of kindness is on her tongue.—Prov. xxxi, 26.

192. *Spiritual Peace*: May the Lord grant thee peace.—Numbers vi, 26.

193. *Strife*: It is an honor for a man to cease from strife.—Prov. xx, 3.

194. *Submission*: Do Thou unto us whatsoever seemeth good unto Thee.—Judges x, 15.

195. *Superstitions*: For all that do these things are an abomination unto the Lord.—Deut. xviii, 12.

196. *Tale-bearing*: Thou shalt not go about as a tale-bearer among thy people.—Levit. xix, 16.

197. *Temptation*: O that Thine hand might be with me, and that Thou wouldst keep me from evil, that it may not grieve me.—I. Ch. iv, 10. (The prayer of Jabez.)

198. *Thankfulness*: Give thanks unto the Lord, for He is good; for His mercy endureth for ever.—Ps. cxxxvi, 1.

199. *Thanksgiving*: Enter into His gates with thanksgiving and into His courts with praise; be thankful unto Him and bless His name.—Psalm c, 4.

200. *Tithes*: Every tithe is holy unto the Lord.—Levit. xxvii, 30.

201. *Transgressors*: The way of the transgressors is hard.—Prov. xiii, 15.

202. *Truth*: Speak the truth, every one to his neighbor.—Zech. viii, 16.

203. *Trust*: Trust in the Lord with all thine heart, and lean not unto thine own understanding.—Prov. iii, 5.

204. *Unbelief*: It is the fool who saith in his heart there is no God.—Psalm xiv, 1.

205. *Ungodly, The*: Should thou help the ungodly, and love them that hate the Lord?—2 Chron. xix, 2.

206. *Universal adoration of God*: I have sworn by Myself, the word is gone out from My mouth in righteousness, and shall not return. That unto Me every knee shall bend, every tongue swear loyalty.—Isa. xlv, 23.

207. *Universal acknowledgment of God*: All the kingdoms of the earth shall know that Thou art the Lord God, even Thou alone.—Isa. xxxvii, 20 and 2 Kings xix, 19.

208. *Universal Brotherhood*: Have we not all One Father? Hath not One God created us?—Mal. ii, 10.

209. *Universal Happiness*: And they shall sit every man under his vine and under his fig-tree, and none shall make them afraid; for the mouth of the Lord of Hosts hath spoken it.—Micah iv, 4.

210. *Universal Kingdom of God*: And the Lord shall be king over all the earth: in that day shall there be One Lord, and His Name One.—Zech. xiv, 9.

211. *Universal knowledge of God*: The earth shall be filled with the knowledge of The Lord as the waters cover the sea.—Isa. xi, 9.

212. *Universal Peace*: Nation shall not lift up sword against nation, neither shall they learn war any more.—Isa. ii, 4 and Micah iv, 3.

213. *Universal service of God*: For then will I turn to the peoples a pure language, that they may all call upon the name of the Lord, to serve Him with one consent.—Zeph. iii, 9.

214. *Universal worship of God*: All shall worship Him, every one from his place, even all the isles of the Gentiles.—Zeph. ii, 11.

215. *Wickedness*: They that plow iniquity and sow wickedness, reap the same.—Job iv, 8.

216. *Wicked imaginations*: The Lord hateth the heart that deviseth wicked imaginations.—Prov. vi, 18.

217. *Willing worship*: When ye offer a sacrifice of thanksgiving unto the Lord, offer it willingly.—Lev. xxii, 29.

218. *Wind-sowing*: They have sown the wind, they shall reap whirlwind.—Hoshea viii, 7.

219. *Wine*: Wine is a mocker.—Prov. xx, 1.

220. *Wisdom*: Wisdom is the principal thing, therefore get wisdom; with all thy getting get understanding.—Prov. iv, 7.

221. *Womanly work*: The good woman worketh willingly with her hands.—Prov. xxxi, 13.

222. *Word*: A word in due season, how good it is.—Prov. xv, 23.

223. *Word, Good*: A good word maketh the heart of a man glad.—Prov. xii, 25.

224. *Worship*: Worship the Lord in the beauty of holiness.—Psalm xxix, 2; xcvi, 9.

225. *Wrong*: Do no wrong.—Jer. xxii, 3.

226. *Youth*: It is good for a man that he bear the yoke in his youth.—Lam. iii, 27.

46

CEREMONIAL LAW (CONTINUED)

Besides those ceremonies to which we have already referred, there are certain others, similarly designed to teach conduct or build character. The chief ones are as follows:

ENROLMENT OR INITIATION INTO THE COVENANT OF GOD.

1. This covenant is called the Covenant of Abraham (Berith Abraham), because God first made it with Abraham. It contains three declarations:

1st. God is our God.
2nd. We are to walk before Him and be perfect.
3rd. We are to possess Palestine, "for an everlasting possession."

2. The first declaration teaches us that if God is our God, we owe certain duty to Him. This declaration therefore announces our Duty to God. (*See Chapter v.*)

3. The second declaration teaches us Conduct, or our Duty to our neighbor (Chapters viii and ix) and our Duty to ourselves. (Chapters v, vi, and vii.) We must walk in the way of God, "doing justly and loving mercy, and walking humbly with Him."

4. The third declaration teaches the Duty of Israel among the nations. The possession of Palestine was never intended for the glory or gain of Israel. It was always designed to be a spiritual influence for good upon all mankind, in accordance with God's first message to Abraham "Be a blessing," and in accordance with His frequent promise to him, to Isaac and Jacob, that all the families of earth should be blessed through them. (*See Chapter xxi, 12-15.*)

5. The ceremony of the initiation is to impress the parents with what is

henceforth their most sacred duty on earth, to educate their children in their duties to God, their neighbor, and themselves. They are responsible to God that they bring up their children as true Israelites, to witness for God (*See Chapter xi, 10-17*), by setting the example of right conduct to Hebrews and to non-Hebrews, at all times and under all circumstances.

6. Boys are received into the covenant on the eighth day after birth, when they receive a name at the same time.

BIBLE QUOTATIONS.

1. And I will establish My Covenant between Me and thee, and thy seed after thee in their generations for an everlasting covenant, to be a God unto thee, and to thy seed after thee.—Gen. xvii, 7.

Walk before Me and be thou perfect.—Gen. xvii, 1.

And I will give unto thee, and to thy seed after thee, the land whereon thou art sojourning, all the land of Canaan, for an everlasting possession, and I will be their God.—Gen. xvii, 8.

2. Ye shall walk after the Lord your God, and reverence Him, and Keep His Commandments, and obey His Voice, and ye shall serve Him and cleave unto Him.—Deut. xiii, 4.

3. He hath shown thee, O man, what is good; and what doth the Lord require of thee, but to do justly, and to love mercy, and to walk humbly with thy God.—Mich. vi, 8.

Thou shalt be perfect with the Lord thy God.—Deut. xviii, 13.

4. Be a blessing.—Gen. xii, 2.

And in thy seed shall all nations of the earth be blessed.—Gen. xxii, 18; xxvi, 4.

5. And thou shalt teach them diligently unto thy children.—Deut. vi, 7.

Set your hearts unto all the words which I testify among you this day, which ye shall command your children to observe to do, all the words of this law.—Deut. xxxii, 46.

For it is not a vain thing for you, for it is YOUR LIFE.—Deut. xxxii, 47.

Ye are My witnesses, saith the Lord, for I am your God.—Isa. xliii, 12.

47

NAMING OF GIRLS.

1. Girls are sometimes named by the father in synagogue, on the Sabbath after their birth.

2. Or they are named at a later day in the home, or in the synagogue at private service, when the minister meets the parents, god-parents, and friends, and blesses the child. The mother thanks God for the child given her to love, and also recites "Hagomel." (*See Chapter xlix, section xv.*)

3. This ceremony, conducted with solemnity, impresses upon the parents their religious duty to their little daughter, to educate her to be a God-fearing woman, valiant for the Right and walking before God, whose way is perfection.

4. Nor may they neglect her training as a Jewess, so that even as Israel among the nations, she, among her Gentile, as well as among her Jewish neighbors, shall be an example in justice, loving-kindness and modesty.

5. Thus the little girl enters the Covenant of God, to become in due time one more witness for God by faithful discharge of her duty to Him, to her neighbor, Jew and Gentile, and to herself.

6. In ancient days, the mother took an offering on her first appearance at the place of worship after the birth of a child. In these days, it is proper that every mother should offer an offering of thanksgiving to God. (*See Hagomel, Chapter xlix, section xv..*)

BIBLE QUOTATIONS.

3. The woman that feareth the Lord, she shall be praised.—Prov. xxxi, 30.
Who can find a virtuous woman? Her price is far above rubies.—Prov. xxxi, 10.

God, His way is perfect.—2 Sam. xxii, 31.

4. On her tongue is the law of kindness.—Prov. xxxi, 26. Strength and honor are her clothing.—Prov. xxxi, 26.

6. And she shall bring an offering unto the door of the tabernacle of the congregation, unto the priest, who shall offer it before the Lord.—Lev. xii, 6. 7.

I will offer to Thee the sacrifice of Thanksgiving, and I will call on the name of the Lord.—Ps. cxvi, 17.

HOME PRAYERS AND CONDUCT REMINDERS.

48

THE READING OF HOME PRAYERS. THE SHEMA', (KERIATH SHEMA',).

1. By this is meant the morning and evening recital of the three sections of the Torah, beginning "Hear, O Israel" (Deut. vi, 4-9). "And it shall come to pass, if ye will hearken diligently" (Deut. xi, 13-21) and "And the Lord spake unto Moses" (Numbers xv, 37-41).

2. They teach the unity of God and the duty of making our love for Him govern our deeds, words, and thoughts (*see Chapter ii to Chapter ix*), the Justice of God (*see Chapter x*), and our duty of obedience to Him, combined with personal purity and consecration to His service. (See *Chapter xi*.)

3. This frequent recital of great teachings of our Religion, if we think of the words as we recite them, cannot fail to influence our conduct and strengthen our characters by awakening us to the Love, Justice, and Holiness of God.

4. The first verses of the Shema' are taught to children from the earliest age. The first verse, the declaration of the Unity of God, is said by every Jew and Jewess on his or her deathbed, and should be recited by those present.

5. Children should be taught to recite appropriate prayers as early as possible. It is of intense importance that their elders, who are present, shall set the example of reverence.

6. The importance of family prayer, led by the father or mother, and conducted with reverence, cannot be over-estimated.

7. To lead our dear ones in prayer is one of the holiest privileges which parents can exercise, and one which should never be surrendered, except to visiting ministers or to friends, whose example may be beneficial to the children.

BIBLE QUOTATIONS.
The Reading of the Shema'.

See Appendix I, II, III.
3. O how I love Thy Law, it is my meditation every day.—Ps. cxix, 97.

O God, Thou art my God, early will I seek Thee.—Ps. lxiii, 1.

To declare Thy loving kindness in the morning and Thy faithfulness every night.—Psalm xcii, 2.

5. Come, O children, hearken unto me, I will teach you the reverence of the Lord.—Psalm xxxiv, 11.

Serve the Lord with reverence.—Psalm ii, 11.

Worship the Lord in the beauty of Holiness.—Psalm xxix, 2.

7. And thou shalt teach thy children diligently.—Deut. vi, 7.

49

GRACE BEFORE AND AFTER MEALS.

1. It is proper to bless God before and after meals. During the Grace or Blessing, as indeed during all religious services, all present should maintain a reverent attitude.

2. The object of this ceremony is to thank God who gives us the means to live, to acknowledge Him as the Creator and Sustainer of all, and to realize that our gratitude is best proved by obedience to His commands.

3. If for material things we should bless God and show gratitude to Him, how much more should we do so for spiritual things and for immortality?

GRACE BEFORE AND AFTER MEALS.

1. And thou shalt eat and be satisfied, and thou shalt bless the Lord thy God.—Deut. viii, 10.

2. Take heed, that thou forget not the Lord thy God .... but when thou hast eaten and art satisfied .... then thy heart be lifted up and thou forget the Lord thy God,.... and thou say in thine heart, my power, and the might of my hand hath gotten me this prosperity.

But thou shalt remember the Lord thy God; for it is He who giveth thee power to acquire prosperity.—Deut. viii, 11, 18.

The Lord will sustain thee.—Psalm lv, 22.

The eyes of all wait upon Thee, and Thou givest them their food in due season.—Psalm cxlv, 15.

Thou openest Thy hand and satisfiest the desire of all living.—Ps. cxlv, 16.

God, who giveth food to the hungry.—Ps. cxlvi, 7.

All things come of Thee.—1 Chron. xxix, 14.

Not by bread alone does man live but by all that proceedeth out of the mouth of the Lord doth man live.—Deut. viii, 3.

Blessed be the Lord who daily loadeth us with benefits.—Psalm lxviii, 19.

3. Come and hear, all ye that fear God, and I will declare what He hath done for my soul.—Ps. lxvi, 16.

50

THE LIGHTING OF THE SABBATH LAMP BY THE MOTHER. (HADLAKATH HA-NER).

(See Chapter xii, The Sabbath, No. 13.)

51

THE SANCTIFICATION OF THE SABBATH BY THE FATHER (KIDDUSH).

(See Chapter xii, The Sabbath, No. 14.)

52

THE "DIVISION" (HAVDALAH), OR CONSECRATION OF THE SENSES FOR THE COMING WEEK'S WORK.

(See Chapter xii, The Sabbath, No. 16.)

53

CONDUCT—REMINDERS. THE FRINGE. (TSITSITH)

1. Just as soldiers wear uniforms, officers wear badges, and free-masons wear aprons, to remind them of certain duties or ideals, so the Tsitsith or Taleth is worn to teach the duty of obedience and the ideal of Holiness.

2. It is meant to be a reminder to obey God's commands, to live pure lives and to consecrate ourselves to God's work. *(See Chapter xi.)*

BIBLE QUOTATIONS.

1. And it shall be unto you for a fringe that ye may look upon it, and remember all the commandments of the Lord, and do them; and that ye seek not after your own heart and your own eyes, after which ye are prone to go astray.—Numbers xv, 39.

2. That ye may remember, and do all My commandments and be holy unto your God.—Numbers xv, 40.

# 54

THE PHYLACTERIES (TEPHILLIN).

1. These are bound on the arm, hand, and brow during morning prayer.

2. The Tephillin, by reason of what they contain, stand for all that is dear and sacred to our religion in the eyes of Hebrews.

3. For they contain four sections of Scripture, each emphasizing fundamental teachings of Judaism, and together expressing the highest ideals of Faith and Conduct.

4. The four sections are as follows:

(a) The section "Hear, O Israel" (Deut. vi, 4-9) teaching the Unity of God, that we must love Him with all our heart, and with all our soul, and with all our might, and that this love for God must govern our words, our deeds, and our thoughts. This, our love for Him, is a result of His love for us. (See Chapters iii to ix.)

(b) The section "And it shall come to pass" (Deut. xi, 13-21) teaching the Justice of God. *(See Chapter x.)*

(c) The section "Sanctify unto Me all the first-born" (Exod. xiii, 1-10). Originally all the first-born in Israel were charged with the religious education of the Hebrews and with ministerial duties. The Levites were subsequently substituted for them. Inasmuch as God calls Israel His first-born, a larger or wider significance is given to this command which makes it mean that all Israel is to be sanctified or consecrated to God.

This consecration to God's service, and for His service, can only be secured by religious education. The example of Abraham illustrates this. Hence the importance of a religious education in the eyes of all Hebrews. Only by such education can we become qualified for consecration, and enabled to teach and practice Right Conduct.

(d) The section "And it shall be when the Lord shall bring thee into the Land" (Exod. xiii, 11-16).

This reference to Palestine carries with it all that the possession of Palestine means; that is, the establishment of a central spiritual influence for the benefit of all mankind, while Hebrews in Palestine and in all countries of the world besides, will teach and practice the ideals of human conduct. *(See Chapters xxi, 11-17; xlii, 12 to end.)*

BIBLE QUOTATIONS.

4(a) see chapters iii to ix.

(b) see chapter x.

(c) Sanctify unto Me all the first-born.—Exod. xiii, 6.

I have taken the Levites instead of all the first-born of the children of Israel.—Numbers viii, 18.

And the priests, the sons of Levi, shall come near; for them the Lord thy God hath chosen to minister unto Him and to bless in the name of the Lord; and by their mouth shall be decided every controversy and every contention.—Deut. xxi, 5.

They (the Levites) shall teach Jacob Thy judgments, and Israel Thy Law.—Deut. xxxiii, 10.

Thus saith the Lord, Israel is My son, my first-born.—Exod. iv, 22.

For I (the Lord) know him (Abraham), that he will command his children and his household after him, and they shall keep the way of the Lord to do righteousness and judgment; that the Lord may bring through Abraham that which He hath spoken concerning him.—Gen. xviii, 19.

(d) From Zion shall go forth the Law and the word of the Lord from Jerusalem.—Isa. ii, 3; Micah iv, 2.

But ye shall be named the Priests of the Lord: men shall call you the Ministers of our God.—Isa. lxi, 6.

And their seed shall be known among the Gentiles, and their offspring among the peoples: all that see them shall acknowledge them, that they are the seed which the Lord hath blessed.—Isa. lxi, 9.

See also chapter viii.

55

THE DOOR-POST INSCRIPTION (MEZUZAH).

(See Chapter ix, 6-9.)

56

BAR-MITZVAH AND THE PASSAGE FROM CHILDHOOD TO YOUTH— CONFIRMATION

THE BAR-MITZVAH.

1. Custom has made thirteen years the age of Bar-Mitzva.
2. Bar-Mitzva means literally "a son of the Commandment"; that is, one who is considered bound to observe the duties of our religion, and who is therefore bound by religious responsibilities.
3. At thirteen years most boys begin to pass from boyhood into youth, the age of new ideas.
4. It is the age of impatience of restraint, when new and strong temptations must be faced, when wrong thoughts must be conquered, wrong impulses resisted, and wrong paths avoided.
5. It is wise therefore to strengthen our sons' characters and prepare them for this age by careful training in moral law.
6. Hence the Bar-Mitzva celebration should always be preceded by conscientious instruction in the moral and spiritual teaching of our religion, besides his other religious duties.
7. This is all important. The mere recital of a section of the Torah in synagogue, by the boy, is of little importance unless his religious education has been well advanced.
8. For some months, therefore, before the day, the lad should study under an instructor able to teach the spiritual beauties of our religious duties and ceremonies.
9. The boy should know at least the Shema', (all three sections); the Ten Commandments, the Creeds, the Holy Days and Festivals, their ethical or spiritual lessons, and the meaning of the Tephillin, Mezuzah and Tsitsith.
10. He should not be permitted to read a portion of the Law in public

unless he can translate it, nor recite the blessings unless he can understand them.

11. The day selected for the Bar-Mitzva celebration is the Sabbath after the boy completes his thirteenth year. In some congregations, especially in the Orient, Monday or Thursday is sometimes selected.

12. Parents and relations should use every effort to add to the solemnity of the occasion, in order that the aspirant may realize his responsibilities.

57

THE RELIGIOUS EDUCATION OF BOYS AND GIRLS.

1. The Religious Education of our sons and daughters is of the highest importance. Only by its thoroughness can they and their children after them, be confirmed in their ancestral faith.

2. Parents should personally instruct their children by Bible Readings. They should personally supervise their religious education and take interest in their Religious School work.

3. Instruction by teachers must be supplemented by personal example at home. This is true Confirmation.

4. The direct religious education of our children is secured by study. The indirect religious education of our children is secured by Home Example.

5. The indirect is more powerful than the direct. The sincerity or insincerity of parents or elders, their attitude of reverence or irreverence during prayer, their observance or neglect of prayer and other religious duties, their respectful or disrespectful remarks about religion and the ministers of religion, will profoundly affect the children and the young men and women of the family, will unfailingly influence their religious nature for good or evil, and will secure their confirmation as real or nominal Jews and Jewesses.

6. Throughout the whole of our lives, our own religious education should be continued. Bible chapters should be read daily. Religious instruction from the matured minds of godly men should be sought in sermon and lecture. In spiritual nature, as in material nature, the more we learn, the more beauties, wonders and possibilities do we discover, and the more we find there is to learn.

7. The religious education of girls is of special importance.

8. Bible intimation as to the age when we are old enough to be considered

responsible, or "firm" in our faith, and, therefore, fit for confirmation, is of interest. In Numbers, xiv, 29, all from twenty years old and upward, are declared responsible for their want of faith in God in the episode of the searching out of Palestine. In Deuteronomy i, 39, alluding to the same episode, those under twenty at that time, are called the ones "who in that day had no knowledge of good and evil." From which some infer that judgment is not sufficiently matured until twenty years of age to confirm one in his ideas.

BIBLE QUOTATIONS.

My son, hear the instruction of thy father, and forsake not the law of thy mother.—Prov. i, 8.

My son, if sinners entice thee, consent thou not.—[Prov. 1,]v. 10.

My son, forget not my law, but let thine heart keep my commandments.—[Prov.] iii, 1.

Remember thy Creator in the days of thy youth.—Ecc. xii, 1.

The thought of folly is sin.—Prov. xxiv, 9.

Let not loving kindness and truth forsake thee: bind them about thy neck: write them upon the table of thine heart.—Prov. iii, 3.

Keep sound wisdom and discretion.—Prov. iii, 21.

Wisdom is the principal thing, therefore get wisdom. And with all thy getting, get understanding.—Prov. iv, 7.

Turn not to the right hand nor to the left: remove thy foot from evil.—Prov. iv, 27.

The way of a fool is right in his own eyes.—Prov. xii, 15.

A foolish son is the calamity of his father.—Prov. xix, 13.

Even a child is known by his doings, whether his work be pure and whether it be right.—Prov. xx, 11.

Every way of a man is right in his own eyes, but the Lord weigheth the hearts.—Prov. xxi, 2.

Train up a child in the way he should go, and when he is old, he will not depart from it.—Prov. xxii, 6.

Bow down thine ear and hear the words of the wise.—Prov. xxi, 17.

Be not one of them that are sureties for debts.—Prov. xxii, 26.

A gracious woman retaineth honor.—Prov. xi, 16.

As a jewel of gold in a swine's nose, so is a fair woman without discretion. —Prov. xi, 22.

Who can find a virtuous woman? Her price is far above rubies.—Prov. xxxi, 10.

She layeth her hands to the spindle, and her hands hold the distaff.—Prov. xxxi, 19.

She stretcheth out her hand to the poor, yea, she reacheth forth her hands to the needy.—Prov. xxxi, 30.

Strength and honor are her clothing.—Prov. xxxi, 25.

She openeth her mouth with wisdom, and on her tongue is the law of kindness.—Prov. xxxi, 26.

She looketh well to the ways of her household, and eateth not the bread of idleness.—Prov. xxxi, 27.

Favor is deceitful, and beauty is vain, but a woman that feareth the Lord, she shall be praised.—Prov. xxxi, 30.

58

CONSECRATION OF THE HOME (CHINUCH-HABAYITH).

1. It is recommended that all new homes be consecrated by the minister.

2. For we all desire God's blessing upon the home. That blessing should be solemnly invoked, and the inmates be thus made to realize the closeness of God to the human being, His fatherly love for His earthly children, and the necessity for them to love their God with all their heart, and with all their soul, and with all their might, if they would have true happiness in the home.

3. The Jewish home is the home wherein God is honored by family prayers at regular times, by the example of reverent demeanor on the part of parents and elders, and by proper and consistent observance of our religious duties, by all, old and young.

BIBLE QUOTATIONS.

1. What man is there that hath built a new house, and hath not dedicated it? Let him go and return unto his house . . . . lest another dedicate it.—Deut. xx, 5.

2. Therefore, now let it please Thee to bless the house of Thy servant, that it may continue for ever before Thee: for Thou, O Lord God, hast spoken it: and with Thy blessing let the house of Thy servant be blessed for ever.—2 Sam. vii, 29.

And the Lord said unto him, I have heard thy prayer and thy supplication, which thou hast made before Me; I have hallowed this house, which thou hast built, to put My name there for ever; and Mine eyes and Mine heart shall be there perpetually.—1 Kings ix, 3.

3. In every place where I make My name to be remembered I will come to thee and bless thee.—Exod. xx, 24.

59

KADDISH OR MEMORIAL PRAYER

1. The Kaddish is a prayer said during the year of mourning for parents, husband or wife, and on the anniversaries of their deaths.

2. It contains no reference to the dead or to death. It is an acknowledgment of the greatness and holiness of God, with a hope for the speedy establishment of His Kingdom. It continues with adoration of God, and concludes with a prayer for peace and life.

Sometimes a prayer for the great and wise of Israel is inserted.

3. The Kaddish means a recognition of the greatness and sanctity of God, in whose holy keeping are our departed loved ones. It leads us thus to a becoming resignation, and thus affords us a comforting consolation.

4. It is also a renewal of our allegiance to the King of Kings, and a testimony to Him, the righteous judge, that our hearts were trained by our parents to be loyal to Him.

BIBLE QUOTATIONS.

But thou shalt go to thy fathers in peace.—Gen. xv, 15.
I shall go to him (my dead child); he will not return to me.—1 Sam. xii, 23.
God of the spirits of all Flesh!—Numbers xxvii, 16.
In His hand is the soul of every living thing, and the breath of all mankind.—Job xii, 10.

60

HAGOMEL OR BLESSING FOR RECOVERY FROM SICKNESS OR FOR ESCAPE FROM ANY GREAT DANGER.

1. Hagomel is a blessing which is said by us whenever we have occasion to thank God for escape from peril or for recovery from sickness.

2. We should either visit the synagogue specially for the purpose, or wait until a regular service is over, or say the blessing when we are called to the reading of the Law.

3. It is said when called to the Reading of the Law, or in front of the ark, which is opened by the husband, or friend, or by the minister who recites certain appropriate selections of prayers or psalms.

4. It is a ceremony which serves to bring nearer to God those who take part therein.

BIBLE QUOTATIONS.

1. What shall I render unto the Lord for all His benefits conferred upon me?—Ps. cxvi, 12.

2. —Offer unto God thanksgiving.—Ps. l, 14.

Come and hear all ye that fear God, and I will declare what He hath done for my soul.

Verily, God heard me; He attended to the voice of my prayer.—Ps. lxvi, 16, 19.

61

PRIVATE PRAYER IN SYNAGOGUE OR TEMPLE.

1. Private prayer can always be offered to God when the place of worship is open for stated service.
2. The place of worship should be accessible all day for those who wish to "seek the Lord" or "to pour out their hearts before Him."

BIBLE QUOTATIONS.

1. And it shall come to pass, that everyone who sought the Lord went out unto the tabernacle of the congregation.—Exod. xxxiii, 7.

2. Pour out your heart before Him: God is a refuge for us.—Psalm lxii, 8.

What prayer and supplication soever be made by any man or by all Thy people Israel, which shall know every one the anguish of his own heart, and spread forth his hands toward this house; Then hear Thou in Heaven, Thy dwelling-place, and forgive and do and give everyone according to his ways, whose heart Thou knowest, for Thou, even Thou only, knowest the hearts of all the children of men.—1. Kings vii, 38, 39.

And Hannah was sore in bitterness of soul, and prayed unto the Lord and wept sore . . . . and she spake in her heart; only her lips moved, but her voice was not heard.—I. Sam. i, 10, 13.

And Hannah prayed and said, My heart rejoiceth in the Lord, mine horn is exalted to the Lord.—I. Sam. ii, 1.

Thy gates shall be open continually, they shall not be shut day or night.—Isa. lx, 11.

Evening and morning and at noon I pray and cry aloud, and He heareth my voice.—Psalm lv, 17.

62

THE DIETARY LAWS

The Dietary Laws are designed:

1st. To keep us holy, and to prevent defilement of the soul.

For gross eating makes a gross nature. And he who cannot hold his appetites in check can never rise to any high standard of conduct.

For I am the Lord your God: ye shall therefore sanctify yourselves, and ye shall be holy; for I am holy, neither shall ye defile your souls with any creeping thing that creepeth upon the earth.—Levit. xi, 44.

2nd. As a means of spiritual discipline, to help to keep our animal appetites in check, and to keep both soul and body pure and free from disease.

"Ye shall therefore make a difference between the clean beast and the unclean, and between the unclean fowl and the clean."—Lev. xx, 25.

3. To enforce our religious separatism.

"And ye shall be holy unto Me, for I, the Lord, am holy and I have separated you from the nations that ye shall be Mine."—Levit. xx, 26.

The Food Laws or Dietary Laws are as follows.

A. Every animal that hath parted hoof and whose feet are cleft into two clefts, and cheweth the cud among beasts—that alone may ye eat.—Levit. xi, 3.

B. All clean fowl may ye eat.—Deut. xiv, 20 or 11.

C. This may ye eat of anything that is in the waters; all that hath fins and scales may ye eat. And whatsoever hath no fins and scales ye shall not eat; it is unclean to you.—Deut. xiv, 9-10. Compare Levit. xi, 9-12.

D. All flying creeping things which have four feet shall be an abomination unto you.—Lev. xi, 23.

E. Every creeping thing that creepeth upon the earth is an abomination, it shall not be eaten.—Levit. xi, 41.

F. Whatsoever goeth upon the stomach and whatsoever goeth upon four feet, down to whatsoever hath many feet among all creeping things that creep upon the earth shall ye not eat, for they are an abomination.—Levit. xi, 42.

G. Ye shall not eat anything that dieth of itself.—Deut. xiv, 21.

H. It shall be a perpetual statute for your generations throughout all your dwellings, that ye eat neither fat nor blood.—Levit. iii, 17.

Moreover ye shall eat no manner of blood in any of your dwellings, whether it be of fowl or of cattle.—Deut. xv, 23.

By these laws we are permitted to eat only clean-feeding animals. All beasts of prey and all whose flesh is apt to be parasitic, all birds of prey and all shell fish are forbidden. The reason for these laws is obvious, especially in the light of modern medical science, which emphasizes the importance of food in relation to the health of the consumers thereof.

As for all shellfish or other scavengers of the sea, we know they flourish especially in or near estuaries of rivers or on coast-lines. It is just there that the sewage of cities is diluted or washed out. This is significant and suggestive enough. To such food have been traced outbreaks of typhoid-fever, etc., as we might well expect, due to typhoid or other germs in the shell-fish.

The connection of such sea-food with certain bodily ailments, especially certain skin diseases, is also recognized.

The wisdom of these Food Laws has frequently been demonstrated by medical science.

With regard to insects and creeping things that feed on refuse, vegetable or animal, they are known to convey disease to the human being by sting, bite or otherwise, or by particles of putrescent matter, or germs adhering to their feet or bodies. To eat such would mean to introduce disease directly into our system. The communicability of the diseases of animals to human beings eating their flesh is recognized to-day as among [the] most serious causes of our ill-health[1].

Blood is frequently and emphatically forbidden. The fact that physicians order blood as medicine does not mean that blood is a proper food. Strychnine, arsenic, and other poisons are also sometimes prescribed. The use of blood as medicine by physicians is diminishing, its evil effects having been found to frequently counterbalance any good results.

The immunity of our race from certain diseases, and its disproportionately high vitality compared with the vitality of other meat-eating races, are undoubtedly due to the care in selection and preparation of food and especially animal food.

We observe the following rules:

1st. Only herbivorous or clean-feeding animals may be eaten.

2nd. The animal is slaughtered in such a way that the blood readily escapes from the body, and the least possible pain is inflicted on the animal. The lungs then are examined for signs of disease, and the whole of the carcass is rejected if such be found. When any piece of meat is carried to a home, it is placed in cold water for at least a half an hour, according to the size; it is then sprinkled generously with salt and remains so salted for one hour; it is afterwards washed off, and only then considered ready for cooking. The immersion in water loosens coagulations and any contamination from handling. The salt draws out blood that may still be in the meat, and kills any noxious germs that may have lodged upon its surface, and the final washing removes them.

We also refrain from using milk, or foods made from milk, with meat of animals.

---

1. Trichina, tapeworm, from eating the flesh of swine, etc., diseases of the liver and other organs from eating lobsters, crabs, etc., are familiar examples.

63

THE ATTITUDE OF JUDAISM TO CHRISTIANITY

The main reasons why we reject Christianity are as follows:

1. Judaism teaches that God is One: a Unity, Christianity teaches that He is three: a trinity.

2. Judaism teaches that God is too good, too just, and too righteous to allow any sinner to escape penalty by another person suffering for him and instead of him. Christianity teaches that Jesus suffered to save mankind.

3. Judaism teaches us to pray to God alone. Christians pray mostly to Jesus or to the Virgin Mary.

4. Judaism commands us to reverence God alone and not to give of His honor to any other being. Christians insult Him by setting aside His Sabbath, the seventh day, in order to show respect to Jesus, in whose honor they keep Sunday as the Sabbath, even though he himself kept the seventh day Sabbath.

5. Judaism teaches that God is our only Saviour. Christianity teaches that Jesus is the saviour of mankind.

6. Judaism teaches that the Messiah must be descended from David, and that in his day, wars shall cease, peace and goodwill shall be established, and the Hebrews will be united in independent government.

As for wars ceasing, since the beginning of the Christian era wars have been constant; peace is always endangered; and goodwill does not and cannot exist while international, civic and commercial jealousies exist as they do.

Nor did the Nazarene unite the Hebrews in independent government by "assembling the outcasts of Israel and gathering together the dispersed of Judah from the four corners of the earth" (Isa. xi, 12).

7. Judaism teaches that every one determines his own life, whether he shall be righteous or sinful. Many Christians believe in Predestination for reward or punishment in future state.

8. Judaism teaches that parents shall not suffer the penalty of children's sins, nor shall children suffer the penalty of parents' sins. Millions of Christians believe that because Adam and Eve sinned in the Garden of Eden, therefore all of us, being descended from them, are sinners. And furthermore, that we cannot be saved from eternal damnation unless we are baptized and believe in Jesus.

9. Judaism does not receive Eternal Punishment as a doctrine: Christianity does.

10. Judaism believes that God is a Spirit, incorporeal, and never assumed human form. Christianity believes that He did assume human form.

The attitude of Judaism to Christianity may be thus further stated:

11. We Hebrews are told that Jesus forbade any change of the Laws and the prophets; that he himself kept the commands of the law of Moses and believed in the prophets; that he never intended to found a new religion.

12. What is called Christianity is a different religion from what he preached and practised. It is a combination of paganism and Judaism, due chiefly to Paul of Tarsus.

13. Hence its adoption of pagan teachings, such as Trinity, Transubstantiation, the appearance of gods in human form, the marriage of divine beings to mortal women, the worship of woman as a goddess, etc.

14. We believe that he obtained followers, some of whom foolishly hailed him as king of the Jews, thus drawing upon him the suspicion and hostility of the Romans, who well knew that the Jews were ripe for rebellion, through the terrible exactions and oppression of the Roman procurator, Pontius Pilate, and his subordinates.

15. That he was induced to claim being Messiah, even though John the Baptist withdrew his countenance from his Messianic pretensions.

16. That he was arrested by the Romans and executed as a possible leader of Jewish rebellion, just as they put to death other leaders of rebellion, such as Theudas.

17. That the story of his trial by the high priest's court is a clumsy invention, for the following reasons:

1. The Jews did not possess the right to inflict capital punishment.
2. The charge that Jesus was Messiah would never be received in a Hebrew court as a criminal offence, whether tacitly or openly made.
3. The charge that he was the Son of God would mean nothing more than the claim of every Jew to be a son of God, who is regarded as our Father.
4. The court could not be held at night.
5. It could not be held at a private or official residence.
6. It could be held only in its regular place—the Lishchath Hagazith (The Court of Hewn Stones).
7. There were four methods of legal execution according to Jewish law. Crucifixion was not one of them.

8. No culprit could be executed on the eve of Sabbath, or Holyday, or Festival.

9. All the evidence against a culprit had to be revised before execution.

According to the Christian account, Jesus was accused of calling himself the son of God, was tried by night in the house of Caiaphas, the high priest, not in the Lishchath Hagazith, was executed by crucifixion on the day of his trial, on the Eve of Sabbath, during the Passover festival, and there was no revision of the evidence.

18. We reject the story that he was three days and three nights in the tomb, for the simple reason that according to their own story, he was entombed on Friday afternoon and the tomb was found empty on Sunday.

19. We reject the story of his resurrection.

1. Because crucifixion kills by starvation and exposure; no vital part is injured; he was too short a time on the cross to die. At most, he could have fainted.

2. That if he really had divine powers, he could have reappeared to confront Pontius Pilate, all the Romans, and all the Jews.

3. That if he was a divine being who had come to save mankind, he could by merely reappearing before the authorities and the people, have effected such a tremendous revolution of thought and revulsion of feeling in his favor, that all would have acknowledged and followed him. The whole Pagan world would have been converted, all the Jews outside of Palestine and within it, would have heard of him and would have followed his religious admonitions. The terrible persecutions of the early Christians by the Pagans would never have taken place, and the yet more terrible and infinitely more shameful persecutions of Jews by Christians would never have blighted the page of human history, would never have outraged and insulted God.

20. We recognize that he has been a teacher of mankind, but we recognize that he was very human and very faulty; witness his misnaming the high priest of Nob, his disrespectful treatment of his mother, his failure to indemnify the owner of a herd of swine whose destruction he caused, his cursing a fig tree because it bore no fruit, his repetition of the falsehood that we Hebrews are taught to hate our enemies, when he must have known that the teachings of our law and sacred writings are to love the non-Hebrew, and to help our enemy. (See quotations appended.)

21. We protest against the Christians supporting their teachings as to Jesus by texts of our Bible, in defiance of history, fact, translation and grammar, for example:

(a) The sceptre shall not depart from Judah, nor a Lawgiver from between his feet until Shiloh come, and unto him shall the gathering of the people be. (Gen. xlix, 10.)

This is the Christian translation, and Christians assert that Jesus was Shiloh, and that the prophecy was fulfilled in him.

As a matter of fact, the sceptre departed from Judah in the year 3338, or 418 years before Jesus was born, when Zedekiah, the last King of Judah, was carried captive to Babylon.

Furthermore, the lawgivers for the Jews for many years before Jesus' birth were the Romans, their conquerors and rulers.

The real interpretation is to be found in I. Kings xi, 29, where Achijah, the prophet from Shiloh, announces that ten of the twelve tribes will depart from the rule of Judah.

Some Jewish authorities translate the passage thus: The sceptre shall not depart from Judah nor a Lawgiver from between his feet for ever. For Shiloh shall come, and to him shall be the gathering of peoples; teaching that Shiloh, by whom Messiah may be meant, will restore the sceptre to Judah, and the right to make laws. This Jesus never did.

(b) "Therefore the Lord Himself shall give you a sign: Behold a virgin shall conceive, and bear a son, and shall call his name Immanuel." (Isa. vii, 14.)

This is the Christian translation, and Christians assert that the virgin was Mary, the mother of Jesus, and that Jesus was the son.

As a matter of historic fact, as the chapter distinctly declares, Rezin, King of Syria, and Pekah, King of Israel, declared war against Ahaz, King of Judah. This was in the year 742 B.C.E. The Lord told Isaiah, the prophet, to go with his son, Shear-Jashub, whose name meant "the remnant will return," and meet and tell King Ahaz to rest quiet and not fear Rezin and the son of Remaliah; "Their plot shall not stand, neither shall it come to pass," verse 7. "Ask thee a sign of the Lord thy God," exclaimed the prophet. "Ask it either in the depth or in the height above." Ahaz did not wish to ask, whereupon the prophet declared the verse, "Therefore the Lord Himself shall give you a sign: Behold, a virgin shall conceive, etc." In the first place, the Hebrew word for virgin is Betulah, not Almah, the word in the text. Secondly, the Hebrew verb is past tense, not future, in the text: "hath conceived," not "shall conceive." The real translation is therefore, "Behold, the young woman hath conceived and will bear a son and shall call his name Immanuel" (verse 14) . . . "Before the child shall know to refuse the evil and choose the good, the land that thou abhorrest shall be forsaken of both her kings."

This actually happened. Before the child could be two years old, the King of Assyria conquered and slew Rezin at Damascus in the year 742 B.C.E. (see II. Kings xvi, 9). And in the year 739 B.C.E. Hoshea slew Pekah (II. Kings, xv, 30; xvii, 1).

The young woman was Isaiah's own wife. "Behold, I and the children whom the Lord hath given me are for signs and for wonders in Israel from the Lord of Hosts who dwelleth in Mount Zion." (Isa. viii, 18.)

Hence one son was named "The Remnant will return"—for "The remnant shall return, even the remnant of Jacob, unto the Mighty God." (Isa. x, 21).

Another was named "Haste booty, speed spoil"; "For before the child shall have knowledge to cry, my father, and my mother, the riches of Damascus, and the spoil of Samaria, shall be taken away before the king of Assyria." (Isa. viii, 4)

As for Immanuel which means God with us, the reason for his name is indicated in verse 8, "the stretching of his (the King of Assyria's) wings shall fill the breadth of the land, O Immanuel," and in verse 10, "it shall come to nought, it shall not stand; for God is with us."

It is difficult to understand why Christians attach the slightest importance to the cited verse as a support of Christian teachings: first because the birth of Jesus 742 years after Ahaz was king, could not have had the slightest possible value as a sign to the king that the alliance and plot of Rezin and Pekah should not stand, for he, and Rezin, and Pekah, would long have ceased to exist.

Secondly, if Jesus was the son of an unmarried woman or virgin, how could he be descended from king David through Joseph, if Joseph was not his father? And further, how could he be Messiah unless so descended?

Thirdly, Jesus was not named Immanuel.

(c) "For unto us a child is born, unto us a son is given, and the government shall be upon his shoulder; and his name shall be called Wonderful, Counsellor, The Mighty God, the Everlasting Father, the Prince of Peace." (Isa. ix, 6.)

This is the Christian translation, and Christians assert that all these titles refer to Jesus.

But the Hebrew verb is active (or Kal), not passive (or Niphal), and therefore means "shall call," not "shall be called."

The real translation is, "And the Wonderful, the Counsellor, the Mighty God, the Everlasting Father, shall call his name Prince of Peace."

That it cannot refer to Jesus, the very verse following sufficiently proves: "Of the increase of his government and peace there shall be no end, upon the throne of David and upon his kingdom, to order it and to establish it with judgment and with justice from henceforth even for ever. The zeal of the Lord of Hosts will perform this."

Jesus never governed, never brought peace, was never associated with the throne of David, nor with his kingdom, never ordered it and never established it.

The Jewish interpretation applies the verse to king Hezekiah, who, as a historic fact, did increase his government and peace, was upon the throne of David, was established in his kingdom, and did establish it with that judgment and justice which mean everlasting establishment—and which would have meant it but for his successors, such as Menassah and Amon.

As for what the zeal of the Lord performed in Hezekiah's day, and how it made his efforts possible by the wonderful rescue from the king of Assyria, the story is too well known to need repetition here.

(d) The famous 53rd chapter of Isaiah is declared by Christians to refer to Jesus.

The 13th verse of the preceding chapter, however, gives the true key to it. Israel, the servant of God, is meant. The chapter tells of Israel's sufferings at the hands of the nations, how he would be despised and rejected, knowing sorrow and acquainted with grief, made to bear persecutions for which the nations would one day grieve, and to carry burdens, the very thought of which would be sorrow to those that imposed them; how they would esteem him stricken, smitten of God, and afflicted; that he would be wounded through brutality and violence that would truly be transgression and iniquity, that he would bear all silently, make his grave with the wicked—(how often he was classed as wicked!)—and be with the rich in his death—(how often his wealth meant his doom!)—yet nevertheless, when his life would be made an offering for sin *i.e.*, when the recognition of his rights by the tardy world would be the world's "offering to the Lord"; (compare chap. lxvi, 20. "And they, the Gentiles, shall bring all your brethren for an offering unto the Lord"); then "he shall see his seed and prolong his days, and the pleasure of the Lord shall prosper in his hand, he shall see of the travail of his soul, and shall be satisfied"; "he will justify many whose iniquities he will endure." "But God will divide him a portion with the great nations, and he shall divide the spoil with the strong; because he poured out his soul to death; and was numbered with the transgressors; and he bare the sin of many and made intercession for transgressors."

We hold that this chapter cannot refer to Jesus, to judge by the comely form and beauty ascribed to him; that he was never esteemed smitten of God; that he could not have been wounded for the transgressions or have been bruised for the iniquities of the myriads born after him; that he did open his mouth when he cried, "My God, my God, why hast Thou forsaken me"; that he did not make his grave with the wicked and was with the rich in his death; but just the reverse, for his grave was with the rich Joseph of Arimathea, and in his death he was executed with two thieves; that his soul was not an offering for sin, for everybody to this day prays for forgiveness for his own sins—a useless proceeding if pre-atoned for; that he did not see his children, for he never had any, and the Hebrew word "seed" is never applied except to actual children; that he did not "prolong his days," for he died young; that the pleasure of the Lord did not prosper in his hand, for his hand was stilled in death with no sign of success, and he did not see any result of his travail.

(e) "Kiss the son, lest he be angry." (Psalm ii, 12.)

This is the Christian translation and Christians refer it to Jesus. As a matter of fact, the Hebrew word Bar is not son, but purity. The Hebrew word for son throughout the whole Bible is always Ben. Hence the verse should be translated "Kiss or embrace purity".

It then agrees with the context, "Be wise now, therefore, O ye kings; be instructed, ye judges of the earth. Serve the Lord with reverence, and rejoice with trembling. Embrace Purity, lest He be angry," etc.

22. We trust the day will speedily dawn when Christians will follow more closely the religion which Jesus knew, preached and practised.

BIBLE QUOTATIONS.

Hear, O Israel, the Lord is our God, the Lord is One.—Deut. vi, 4.

1. I am God, there is none else; I am God, there is none like Me.—Isa. xlvi, 9.

(For other quotations declaring that our God is the only God, and that there is no God with Him or besides Him, see *Chapters iii, xxxiii*.)

2. The fathers shall not be put to death for the children, neither shall the children be put to death for the fathers. Every man shall be put to death for his own sin.—Deut. xxiv, 16.

The soul that sinneth, it shall die. The son shall not bear the iniquity of the father, neither shall the father bear the iniquity of the son; the righteousness of the righteous shall be upon him, and the wickedness of the wicked shall be upon him.—Ezek. xviii, 20.

And the Lord said unto Moses, Whosoever has sinned against Me, him will I blot out of My book.—Ex. xxxii. 33.

3. Thou shalt reverence the Lord thy God, Him shalt thou serve, and to Him thou shalt cleave and thou shalt be loyal to His name.—Deut. x, 20.

He is thy praise, and He is thy God.—Deut. x, 21.

Ye shall not go after other gods, of the gods of the people which are around you.—Deut. vi, 14.

Ye shall not reverence other gods, nor bow yourselves to them, nor serve them. . . .

But the Lord . . . Him shall ye reverence, and Him shall ye worship.—II Kings xvii, 35, 36.

Ye shall not reverence other gods.—II Kings xvii, 37.

I am the Lord; That is My Name; and My glory I will not give to another.—Isa. xlii, 8.

4. How shall My name be polluted? I will not give My glory unto another.—Isa. xlviii, 11.

The seventh day is the Sabbath of the Lord, thy God.—Ex. xx, 10.

Verily My Sabbaths ye shall keep.—Ex. xxxi, 13.

On the seventh day is the Sabbath of rest, holy to the Lord.—Ex. xxxi, 15.

My honor I will not give to another.—Isa. xlii, 8.

He is my Saviour.—II Sam. xxii, 3.

They forgot God, their Saviour.—Ps. cvi, 21.

For I am the Lord, thy God, the Holy One of Israel, thy Saviour.—Isa. xliii, 3.

O God of Israel, the Saviour.—Isa. xlv, 15.

There is no God else besides Me, a just God and a Saviour; there is none besides Me.—Isa. xlv, 21.

I, even I, am the Lord, and besides Me, there is no Saviour.—Isa. xliii, 11.

Look unto Me, and be ye saved, all the ends of the earth; for I am God, and there is none else.—Isa. xlv, 22.

Thou shalt know no God but Me for there is no Saviour besides Me.—Hos. xiii, 4.

6. And there shall come forth a rod out of the stem of.8. Jesse, and a branch shall grow out of his roots.—Isa. xi, 1.

They shall not hurt nor destroy in all My Holy mountain; for the earth shall be full of the knowledge of the Lord, as the waters cover the sea.—Isa. xi, 9.

And he shall set up an ensign for the nations, and shall assemble the outcasts of Israel, and gather together the dispersed of Judah from the four corners of the earth.— Isa. xi, 12.

7. See, I set before thee this day life and good, and death and evil.—Deut. xxx, 15.

I call heaven and earth to witness this day against you, that I set before you life and death, blessing and blighting: therefore, choose life that both thou and thy seed may live.—Deut. xxx, 19.

8. See No. 2.

10. See *Ch. xxxiv.*

20. "Thou shalt not hate thy brother in thy heart."—Lev. xix, 17.

The Jewish Attitude to Non-Jews and to Enemies.

"Love the stranger."—Deut. x, 19.

"If thou meet thine enemy's ox or his ass going astray, thou shalt surely bring it back to him again."—Ex. xxiii, 4.

"If thou see the ass of him that hateth thee lying under his burden and wouldst forbear to help him, thou shalt surely help him."—Ex. xxiii, 5.

"I should have denied the God that is above if I rejoiced at the destruction of him that hateth me or exulted when evil overtook him."—Job xxxi, 28, 29.

Rejoice not when thy enemy falleth, and let not thine heart be glad when he stumbleth.—Prov. xxiv, 17.

"If thine enemy be hungry, give him bread to eat, and if he be thirsty, give him water to drink. For thou shalt heap coals of fire upon his head, and the Lord will reward thee."—Prov. xxv, 21, 22.

APPENDICES

APPENDIX I.

The First Portion of the Shema'.
(Deut. vi, 4-9.)

1. Hear O Israel, the Lord is our God, the Lord is One.
2. Blessed be the name of the glory of His Kingdom forever and ever.
3. And thou shalt love the Lord thy God with all thy heart and with all thy soul and with all thy might.
4. And these words which I command thee this day shall be in thy heart.
5. And thou shalt teach them diligently unto thy children and thou shalt speak of them when thou sittest in thy house, and when thou walkest by the way, and when thou liest down and when thou risest up.
6. And thou shalt bind them for a sign upon thy hand and they shall be as frontlets between thy eyes.
7. And thou shalt write them upon the door-posts of thy house and upon thy gates.

APPENDIX II.

The Second Section of the Shema'.
(Deut. xi, 13-21.)

And it shall come to pass, if ye will hearken diligently unto my commandments which I command you this day, to love the Lord your God and to serve Him with all your heart and with all your soul.

Then will I give you rain for your land in its due season, the first rain, and the latter rain, that thou mayest gather in thy corn, thy wine, and thy oil.

And I will give grass in thy field for thy cattle, that thou mayest eat and be satisfied.

Take heed to yourselves lest your heart deceive and ye turn aside and serve other gods, and worship them.

For then the Lord's wrath shall be kindled against you, and He will shut up the heavens, that there be no rain, and the land will not yield her produce, and ye shall quickly perish from off the goodly land which the Lord giveth you.

Therefore shall ye lay up these My words in your heart and in your soul, and ye shall bind them for a sign upon your hand, and they shall be as frontlets between your eyes.

And ye shall teach them to your children speaking of them when thou sittest in thy house, when thou walkest by the way, and when thou liest down, and when thou risest up.

And thou shalt write them upon the door-posts of thy house, and upon thy gates.

That your days may be multiplied, and the days of your children, in the land which the Lord promised unto your fathers to give them as the days of heaven upon the earth.

APPENDIX III.

The Third Section of the Shema'.
(Numbers xv, 37-41.)

And the Lord spake unto Moses, saying: Speak unto the children of Israel, and bid them make for themselves a fringe on the borders of their garments, throughout their generations, and that they put upon the fringe of the borders a thread of blue.

And it shall be unto you for a fringe, that ye may look upon it and remember all the commandments of the Lord, and do them, and that ye seek not after the inclination of your heart and after your eyes, after which ye go astray.

That ye may remember and do all My commandments and be holy unto your God.

I am the Lord your God who brought you out of the land of Egypt, to be your God. I am the Lord your God.

APPENDIX IV.

The Months.

The Ecclesiastical Year begins with Nissan. Nissan is thus called the beginning of the months. From it the months of the festivals are reckoned.

The New Year for Trees falls on 15th Shebat. From that date was reckoned the age of a newly-planted tree for the fifth year, when its fruit might be eaten, and for tithing purposes.

The Hebrew months are as follows: Nissan, Iyar, Sivan, Tamuz, Ab, Elul, Tishri, Heshvan, Kislev, Tebet, Shebat and Adar. Hebrew months are lunar months of 29½ days. In order to equalize the lunar year with the solar year, an extra month is added in certain years. This extra month follows Adar, which is then called Adar Rishon, or First Adar, and the extra month is called Adar Sheni, or Second Adar. Purim, etc., and anniversaries are then observed in Adar Sheni.

APPENDIX V.

Jewish Glossary[1]

Aceite.—Lit. oil. *Spanish.* An offering of oil for the Ner Tamid (which see), usually in memory of the dead. *Portuguese* Azeite The term is used by the Sephardim (which see).

Afikomen.—A special Matsa for the Passover-Eve Home Service (Seder). A half of it is shared at the end of the meal among all participants in order that the meal should end with eating Matsa. Some keep a piece of it throughout the year to remind them that just as God provided for and protected our ancestors, so will He provide for and protect us. The Matsa is thus made a symbol of Divine protection and providence.

Alav (mas.) or Aleah (fem.) Hashalom.—Peace be to him or peace be to her. An expression used on mentioning the name of a deceased person.

Aleah.—A calling up to the reading of the Law.

Amen.—Verily. May it be so.

Am Haaretz.—(Lit. People of the earth) *i. e.*: peasants or uneducated people.

Amidah.—(Lit. Standing.) A special prayer said by the congregation while standing. (See Shemone Esre.)

Anusim.—(Lit. Compelled.) Those compelled to keep their religion secret.

Arba' Kanfoth.—(Lit. Four corners.) A four cornered garment with fringes attached. (See Tsitsith, Chapter 11.)

Arbith.—Evening Service.

Aron Hakodesh.—(Lit. Holy Ark.) The depository of the Scrolls of the Law.

Ascabah.—(Properly Hashcava.) Memorial Prayer.

ASHKENAZIM.—Hebrews residing in, or descended from those who resided in Germany, Russia, Poland, Hungary, Galicia, Roumania and other countries of Central Europe. From Ashkenaz, grandson of Japheth, son of Noah (Gen. x, 2-3), who is said to have settled in Central Europe.

AVEL.—Mourner.

BAAL HABAYITH.—(Lit. Master of the House.) The head of the Jewish home who has certain religious responsibilities. (See preceding chapters, on Sabbath, Passover, Enrolment, Education of Boys and Girls, etc.)

BAAL KORE.—(Lit. Reader.) A reader of the Law.

BAAL TOKEA.—The one who sounds the Shofar.

BENSCHING.—A corruption of the Jewish German *benschen*, which in itself is probably a corruption of the Latin *benedicere*, to bless. The term is used to apply especially to the Grace after Meals.

BERITH MILAH.—The initiation into the Abrahamic covenant.

BESIMAN TOB.—May it be in good season.

BETH DIN.—(Lit. House of Judgment.) A tribunal composed of three rabbis to decide cases of Jewish law. Each member of the court is called a Dayan or judge.

BETH HAKENESETH.—(Lit. House of assembly.) A synagogue.

BETH HAIM.—(Lit. House of Life.) The burial ground.

BETH HAMEDRASH.—(Lit. House of instruction.) A place for Jewish study.

BEDIKATH CHAMETS.—(Lit. Search for leaven.) The searching of the house the night before the eve of Passover for leaven to be burned the next morning. (See Chametz.)

BLOOD ACCUSATION.—A wickedly false charge, made even in these days, against the Jews in certain countries declaring that Jews use blood for ritual purposes during Passover. It is sometimes said that the custom of throwing open the doors wide as we finish the evening meal in the home Passover service is to court investigation and so prove the falsity of the charge.

BURIAL.—The rabbis, many centuries ago, emphasized the use of simple linen burial garments. Expense which cannot benefit the dead is to be avoided; though there is no limit to the expense which may be incurred to do good *in memory of* the dead. A great aim of Jewish burials is to prevent any distinction between poor and rich.

CABBALA.—(Lit. Tradition.) A mystic philosophy of the mediaeval Jews, for many years taught only traditionally.

CALLING TO THE LAW (Aleah).—It is considered a special privilege to be called to the Law to hear a portion of it read therein. Formerly the person called would himself read the portion. The respect that is shown to the Law by parents and elders is an object lesson of reverence and loyalty for the child.

CARRERA.—(Lit. Row.) The rows of graves in the Beth Haim. (Sephardic.)

CAUTIVOS.—(Lit. Captives.) A fund for the ransom of those captured by pirates. (Sephardic.) Jewish merchants and travellers were frequently captured in the Mediterranean up to the last century.

CENSOR.—A state officer appointed to supervise the publication of Jewish books, and especially the Talmud, in order to eliminate anything offensive to Christians.

CHALAH.—A special loaf for the Sabbath or Festivals, fancifully covered with seeds to represent manna, and laid between two cloths to represent the dew. In making bread, many Jewesses throw a small piece of dough into the fire in memory of an ancient offering.

CHALDAIC.—A language or dialect anciently used by the oriental Jews.

CHAMETZ.—(Lit. Leaven.) A term applied to any leaven or fermented food.

CHATAN.—(Sometimes pronounced Chosun.) A bridegroom.

CHAYIM.—(Life) or Chayim Tobim (Good Life) Lechayim (For Life). A salutation. The second is said by the Sephardic Hebrews where German Hebrews say *Gesundheit*; i. e.: after sneezing, sneezing being regarded as a possible precursor of illness. I have heard it said that it was one of the symptoms of the terrible black plague. The Sephardic response is *Yosephu lecha shenoth hayim*, May you have many years.

CHAZAN.—A cantor or reader of the service.

CHAZANUTH.—Pertaining to the office of Chazan.

CHEDER.—(Lit. Room.) A Hebrew School.

CHEREM.—(Lit. Separation.) A sentence of excommunication pronounced against those causing public scandal.

CHEVRA.—An association or society for religious and benevolent purposes.

CHEVRA KADISHA.—(Lit. Holy Society.) A society whose members prepare the dead for burial, which is considered a privilege and a sacred duty.

CHIEF RABBI.—The Chief or Presiding Rabbi of a Community. And this authority is practically extended over all.

CHILUL HASHEM.—(Lit. a profanation of the Name.) Any disgraceful act. For it brings shame upon the guilty person and profanes the name of God, whose servant he ought to be.

CHOL HAMOED.—The middle days of the Festivals.

CHOMETZ BATTLEN.—Annulment of Leaven.

CHUMISH.—(Lit. fifth.) A term applied to the Pentateuch.

CHUKOTH HAGOYIM.—Lit. Religious Customs of the Gentiles.

CHUPA.—A wedding canopy.

COHEN.—A descendent of the family of Aaron, hence of the caste of high priests.

COUNTING THE OMER.—See Chap. xvi, 17. The days are called "Sephira," or "counting."

DARSHAN.—(Lit. A searcher.) A preacher.

DARUSH.—A sermon. (Sephardim.)

DEROSHO.—A sermon. (Ashkenazim.)

DIN.—(Lit. Judgment.) A law or legal decision.

DUCHAN.—(Lit. Platform.) The benediction by the Cohanim, pronounced on the platform in front of the Ark.

ERUB.—Certain rabbinical modifications due to the advent of Sabbath, such as the extension of the traditional Sabbath. Day journey for a Mitsvah; or the preparation of food for the Sabbath on the Holy Day preceding; it is then called the Erub Tavshillin.

GAN EDEN.—The Garden of Eden. The paradise of the future world.

GAON.—(Lit. Excellent.) Originally a learned Rabbi of Babylonia. Plural, *Gaonim.* Now used for any rabbi of exceptional learning.

GEHINNOM.—See Chapter on meaning of the 13th Creed.

GELILAH.—(Lit. Rolling up.) The rolling up of the Scroll of the Law. Any office connected with the Law is considered an honor.

GEMARA.—The comment or completion of the Mishna. The Mishna and Gemara together form the TALMUD (which see).

GEMILUTH CHESED.—(Lit. Bestowal of Mercy.) Any act of charity or love.

GER.—(Lit. Stranger.) A proselyte.

GET.—(Lit. A document of divorce.) A divorce.

HAGADAH.—(Lit. The telling.) The home service of the first two nights of the Passover. Also the interpretation of the Talmud as contrasted with the legal interpretation of the Halacha.

HAGBAA.—(Lit. Elevation.) The elevation of the Law in the synagogue.

HAHAM.—(Lit. A wise man.) Same as Chief Rabbi (which see.) (Sephardim.)

HALLEL.—(Lit. Praise.) Psalms cxiii-cxviii.

HAPHTARAH.—A section of the Prophets, read on the Sabbath, Holydays, Fast of Ab, etc., usually referring in some way to the Scriptural portion of the day.

HATARATH HORAAH.—Permission to teach. A certificate or diploma as a rabbi.

HECHAL.—(Lit. Shrine.) The Ark or repository of the Scrolls.

HESPED.—(Lit. Mourning.) A mourning service usually with one or more orations in honor of the noteworthy dead.

ISRU CHAG.—The day following the three great festivals.

JAHRZEIT.—(Lit. Anniversary.) The anniversary of the death of a parent, etc. (See Nahala.)

JEWS.—Literally and originally members of the tribe of Judah, then members of the kingdom of Judah which included the two tribes of Judah and Benjamin. The kingdom of Judah was so called to distinguish it from the kingdom of Israel, which comprised the other ten tribes. In later days, as now, the term is applied to the Hebrews or Israelites.

JUEDISCH DEUTSCH.—A jargon of the Askenazim.

JUBILEE.—Every fiftieth year. (See Leviticus, Chapter xxv.)

KAHAL or KEHILAH.—A congregation.

KAHAL KADOSH.—A holy congregation.

KALLA.—A bride.

KALOTH ROSH.—Uncovered head. Used also to mean levity in conduct.

KASHER.—(Lit. Fit or clean.) Food fit to be eaten according to Jewish law or custom.

KETHUBA.—(Lit. Writing.) A Document, especially a marriage deed or contract.

Kiddush Hashem.—(Lit. Hallowing of the Name.) Any act that redounds to the glory of God.

Kinoth.—Lamentations, dirges.

Kol Nidre.—A remission of certain vows, said before Kipur evening service.

Kosher.—(See Kasher.)

Ladino.—An old Spanish-Hebrew dialect, still spoken by the Sephardim.

Lag B'Omer.—(Lit. 33d in Omer.) The 33d day of the Omer (See Chap. xvi), on which day certain religious restrictions are removed. (Lag la-omer, Sephardim.)

Lavadores.—Those who wash the dead. (Sephardic.)

Lashon Hakodesh.—(Lit. Holy Language.) The Hebrew language.

Leshanah Tovah.—(Lit. For a Good Year.) A New Year Greeting.

Levantadores.—(Lit. Raisers.) Those who raise the Law. (Sephardic.) (See Hagbaa.)

Levi, Levite.—Descendants of the tribe of Levi.

Luach.—(Lit. Table.) The table of dates, or calendar.

Maariv.—The evening service.

Machzor.—(Lit. Cycle.) The prayer books for Holydays and Festivals.

Maftir.—The one who reads the last verses of the weekly portion of the Law and who usually reads the Haphtarah.

Magen David.—(Lit. Shield of David.) Two equilateral triangles, interlaced.

Magid.—(Lit. Teller.) A preacher, usually one who preaches in Juedisch-Deutsch with many illustrations.

Mahamad.—(Lit. Standing.) The wardens, trustees, of council of elders. Sephardic.

Mappa.—The band of the Sefer Torah.

Marrano.—A secret Jew. (Sephardic.)

Mashal.—A fable or proverb or verbal illustration.

Massora.—(Lit. Tradition.) The labors of the Massorites (6th to 10th centuries) to preserve the Hebrew text of the Bible.

Medrash.—(Lit. Explanation.) The collection of expositions of the Pentateuch, etc.

Megilla.—(Lit. A scroll.) Properly anything written on a scroll. Any of the five books Ruth, Song of Solomon, Ecclesiastes, Lamentations and Esther, especially the last-named.

Meshumad.—A convert from Judaism.

Mincha.—Afternoon service.

Minhag.—Custom.

Minyan.—(Lit. Number.) Ten, the legal quorum for a regular religious service.

Mishna.—The compilation of oral law by Rabbi Jehudah the Prince (about the year 200 C.E.).

Mitsvah.—(Lit. Command.) Any religious duty.

Mizrach.—The East.

MUSAPH.—Additional Service.

NAHALA.—(Lit. Inheritance.) Anniversary, or Yahrzeit. A Hebrew term used by Sephardim.

NEILA.—Concluding service of Kipur.

NER TAMID.—(Perpetual Lamp.) The lamp in front of the Ark, in memory of the Temple Lamp. (See Ex. xxvii, 20, 21.) Also regarded as a memorial of the dead, for which reason many send oil for it on the anniversaries of their bereavements.

OMER.—See Chap. xvi, 15.

PARASHA.—The portion of the Pentateuch for Sabbaths or Holy Days.

PARNAS.—A presiding officer, warden or trustee.

PAROCHETH.—A curtain.

PASKEN.—To decide questions of Jewish Law.

PASUL.—Any thing unfit for Jewish use.

PESACH SHENEE.—A second Passover, observed on the 15th Iyar by those unable to keep it on the 15th of Nisan, for reasons indicated in Numbers, ix: 9-14.

PIDYON HABEN.—(Lit. Redemption of the First Born.) In memory of the first born being relieved from ministerial service, a nominal payment of five small pieces of silver is made to a Cohen, who usually gives it for charity; just as a fixed sum is given to be relieved from conscription or other duties.

PILPUL.—Minute discussion.

PIYUTIM.—Poems, metrical compositions introduced into the liturgy.

PORGING.—Removal of the thigh-sinew, forbidden fat, and certain veins.

RABBI.—(Lit. My master.) A master in Jewish law.

RASHA'.—A wicked person.

ROSH HODESH.—(Lit. Head of the Month.) The first day of the month.

SATAN.—(Lit. Adversary.) Anyone who hinders.

SEDER.—The home service of the first two nights of Passover.

SEDRA.—The weekly portion.

SEFER TORAH.—The Scroll of the Law.

SEGAN.—The vice-president, or second warden or trustee.

SELICHOTH.—The Penitential Prayers.

SEMICHA.—(Lit. Laying on.) The placing of hands. Part of the ancient ceremony of Rabbinical Ordination.

SEPHARDIM.—Hebrews residing in Spain and Portugal, or descendants of Hebrews who resided there.

SEPHARAD (Obad. i, 20) is identified by many with Spain.

SEVEN BLESSINGS.—Applied to the seven blessings at the wedding ceremony.

SHAANAS BEATING.—A rough method of waving the willow boughs in festive joy, at the close of the harvest festival.

SHAATNEZ.—The mixture of linen and wool, which is forbidden. (Deut. xxii, 11.)

SHACHRITH.—The Morning Prayer.

SHABBATH HAGADOL.—(Lit. The great Sabbath.) The Sabbath before Passover.

SHABBATH SHUVAH.—(Lit. The Sabbath of Repentance.) The Sabbath before Kipur.

SHALOM.—Peace. A Jewish greeting.

SHALOM ALECHEM.—Peace be unto you.

SHAMAS.—The sexton or beadle of the Synagogue.

SHECHINAH.—The Divine Presence.

SHECHITAH.—(Lit. Slaughter.) The Jewish method of slaughtering animals.

SH'LIACH TSIBBUR.—(Lit. Messenger of the Congregation.) The officiating reader.

SHELOSHIM.—(Lit. 30.) The thirty days of special mourning after the funeral.

SHEMONE ESRE.—(Lit. 18.) The eighteen blessings, which constitute the chief Jewish prayer following the Shema'. They are short prayers, one or more of which must appeal to every worshipper under all circumstances. Another prayer was added about the second century, as a precaution against informers or Minim.

SHEOL.—The grave.

SHIVA.—Seven. The seven days of deep mourning after the funeral.

SHOCHET.—(Lit. Slaughterer.) A man licensed to kill animals according to Jewish law.

SHOOL.—Properly Schule. (A school.) A Synagogue.

SHULCHAN ARUCH.—A Code of Jewish law by Rabbi Karo, derived from the Tur of Rabbi Jacob Asheri, which is in turn a codification of Talmud laws. (1565 C. E.)

SHUSHAN PURIM.—The day following Purim.

SIDUR.—(Lit. Order.) Order of prayers or prayer-book.

SNOGA.—Abbreviation of Sinagoga (Spanish and Portuguese). A Synagogue (Sephardic).

SOPHER.—A scribe.

TAHARA.—(Lit. Purification.) The washing of a corpse.

TALMUD.—The Mishna and Gemara, or complete commentary explaining our religion. The Jerusalem Talmud was completed about the year 370 C. E. The Babylonian Talmud was completed about 500 C. E.

TARGUM.—The Aramaic translation of the Bible.

TARYAG.—(Lit. 613.) The number of commands, 365 of which are negative and 248 positive.

TEBAH.—(Lit. Ark.) Used by the Sephardim to mean the reading desk.

T'NACH.—A word composed of the first letters of the Torah, Nevi-im, Chetuvim, or Law, Prophets and Holy Writings; and used therefore to mean the whole Bible.

TEN WORDS.—The Decalogue or Ten Commandments.

TEVILAH.—Immersion prescribed for converts, etc., doubtless the origin of Baptism.

TERRA SANTA.—The Sacred Earth. Earth or dust from Palestine, a little of which is placed in the coffin before closing it. This custom is more general among the Sephardim than among the Ashkenazim. It symbolizes the love for the sacred soil of Palestine.

TREPHA.—(Lit. Torn.) Any food not fit, according to Jewish law, to be eaten.

TSADIK.—A righteous person.

TSARA.—Sorrow.

TSEDAKAH.—Righteousness or charity.

VIDUI.—Confession.

WASHING THE HANDS.—A custom observed before meals, before prayer, or on leaving the burial ground. One of the Jewish methods of insisting upon cleanliness and purification.

WINE GLASS AT WEDDING.—A wine glass is shattered by the bridegroom after the ceremony. The usual explanation is that it is to remind us of the shattered glory of our nationality, the thought of which should never be absent from our minds, even in the moment of greatest joy.

YETSER HARA'.—The evil imagination, or impulse.

YETSER HATOV.—The good imagination or impulse.

YOM TOV.—(Lit. Good Day.) A Jewish Holy Day.

ZACHUR LETOV.—May it be remembered for good.

ZICHRONO LIVRACHA.—May his memory be blessed.

---

1. There are so many methods of pronouncing Hebrew words that it is impossible to spell them with English letters in a way that can be acceptable to all Hebrews.

    For example, Chatan (which see) is Chosun with the Ashkenazim, Chatan with Sephardim Jews.

    Chukoth Hagoyim is Chukos Hagoyim with most Ashkenazim, Chukows Hagow-yim with English Ashkenazim, Chukot Hagoyim with most Sephardim, Chukoth Hagoyim with some.

    Cohen is pronounced as written by all Sephardim and by all Ashkenazim except the English Ashkenazim, who pronounce the word Cow-hine.

    The familiar Amen is pronounced Ah-men by most Sephardim, A-min by others. Most of the Ashkenazim pronounce it O-men; others pronounce it O-main, and the English Ashkenazim pronounce it O-mine.

COPYRIGHT

Copyright © 2019 by FV Éditions
Cover : Pixabay.com, FVE
All rights reserved.

Also Available

THE TORAH

www.ingramcontent.com/pod-product-compliance
Lightning Source LLC
LaVergne TN
LVHW091542070526
838199LV00002B/172